AFTER THE PINES

ITASCA COUNTY'S QUASQUICENTENNIAL

BY
Jody Hane

With the Itasca County
Historical Society Book Committee:

Leona Litchke, Barb Adams, Esther Hietala,
Jeremy Anderson, and Lilah Crowe

Copyright © 2016 by the Itasca County Historical Society.

No part of this publication may be reproduced, stored in a retrieval system or transmitted in any way by any means, electronic, mechanical, photocopy, recording or otherwise without prior permission of the author except as provided by USA copyright law.

Library of Congress Control Number: 2016918116

Book design copyright © 2016 by Treasure Bay Printing. All rights reserved.
Cover and interior design by Treasure Bay Printing
Photos property of Itasca County Historical Society

Published in the United States

Table of Contents

Timeline	1
Maps	9
Preface	14
Itasca County	16
La Prairie	21
Grand Rapids	22
Cohasset	30
Trout Lake Township	32
Deer River	33
Iron Range Township	35
Coleraine	36
Taconite	39
Bovey	41
Talmoon	43
Feeley Township	44
Ardenhurst Township	46
Bigfork	47
Effie	49
Nore Township	50
Third River/Good Hope/Moose Park Townships	51
Nashwauk	52
Keewatin	53
Alvwood Township	55
Sago Township	56
Swan River	57
Goodland Township	58
Kinghurst/Grattan/Pomroy Townships	59
Marcell/Stokes Township	61
Suomi	62
Bearville Township	64
Togo	65
Wirt	67
Balsam/Lawrence Townships	69
Arbo Township	71
Greenway Township	73
Marble	74
Calumet	76
Blackberry Township	77
Harris Township	78
Wawina Township	80
Spang Township	81
Cooley	82
Pengilly	84
Morse Township	85
Oteneagen Township	86
Bowstring Township	87
Max	88
Squaw Lake	89
Wabana Township	90
Liberty Township	91
Wildwood/Splithand Townships	92
Ball Club	93
Leech Lake Indian Reservations	94
Bois Forte	95
"Ag" School	96
LISTS	
Post Offices	99
Lakes	102
CCC Camps	109
Trains	110
Mines	114
Bars & Saloons	118
Churches	125
Resorts	128
Schools	132
Sheriffs	140
References	144
Glossary	146

QUASQUICENTENNIAL

In 2016, Itasca County Historical Society (ICHS) celebrated Itasca County and Grand Rapids Quasquicentennial with 3 main events: Itasca County and Grand Rapids FIRSTS Exhibit, 125 years of Fashion, and 125 years of Transportation.

Itasca County Historical Society was formed in 1948. It was housed in the Itasca County Courthouse until 1972, when it moved temporarily into Central School. It officially opened a museum in Central School in 1984 where it remained until 2013, when the society purchased the former Corcoran Auto Supply Store in downtown Grand Rapids.

Itasca County Historical Society's mission is to connect people to the history of Itasca County. ICHS has a museum, the Karjala Genealogy and History Research Center, gift shop, offices, and a preservation room for its collection.

TIMELINE

1849   Minnesota Territory established October 27. It was divided into 5 counties. Itasca County formed to include all of Minnesota from Mille Lacs Lake north to Canada, embracing present counties of Itasca, Carlton, Koochiching, Crow Wing, Lake, Cook, St. Louis, eastern Beltrami and parts of Aitkin and Cass Counties.

1850   Population of original Itasca County given by U.S. Government Census Bureau, 97 souls.

1851   Cass County established; 1855 – St. Louis County established; 1857 – Aitkin, Carlton, and Crow Wing Counties established; 1856 – Lake County established; 1874 – Cook County established; 1906 - Koochiching County established.

1854   East and West Pokegama town site laid out on both banks of the Mississippi River at Pokegama Falls, three miles upriver from present Grand Rapids; plat filed in Morrison County, the nearest organized county.

1858   Steamer NORTH STAR, later rechristened the ANSON NORTHRUP, is first steamer to reach Grand Rapids. Minnesota becomes a state on May 11th.

Minnesota 1849 Itasca County

1868   First cut of logs from Pokegama Lake goes down the Mississippi River.

1870   Itasca County census - 96 people. Town of "Long Rapids" became known as "Grand Rapids".

1872   Although logging camps, trading posts and buildings were on the site earlier, the first permanent building was the Potter Company general store. Lowe G. Seavey built the first hotel. Logging began on the Prairie River. Seventeen lumber camps were operating in the area, with 350 to 400 men. Wages in the woods were $16 to $18 per month.

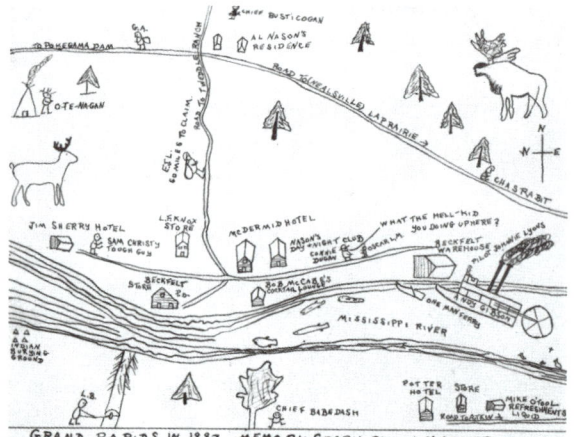

Hand drawn map of early Grand Rapids

1882   Mrs. Katherine C. Lent, first white business woman to settle in Grand Rapids, lived here for 41 years. She was a very prominent business person, owning a millinery shop, a casket shop, a garage, real estate, stock in several logging companies and a copper mine in Arizona.

1883   Hattie Streetar is first white child born in Grand Rapids.

1885   Pokegama Dam begins operating - construction started in 1882.

1887   First school opened in small log building in Grand Rapids. Entire county included in School District No. 1 for school purposes. In 1900, it was the largest school district in area in the United States. Unorganized Itasca County detached from Crow Wing County and attached to Aitkin County for record, tax and judicial purposes.

1

1888	Grand Rapids township organized.
	First farm started by Duncan Harris. There were no farms in Itasca County in 1880 and only 18 in 1890. But, in 1920 the county boasted about 1500 farms, with potatoes as the most valuable crop.
	First schoolhouse built in Grand Rapids. Road from Grand Rapids south to Aitkin constructed.
1889	Bridge built across the Mississippi River at Grand Rapids.
1890	Original Pokegama Hotel built; burned in 1893.
	Village of LaPrairie is incorporated. Located near the mouth of the Prairie River, it developed as a logging community. The steamboat landing on the Mississippi River was first called Neal's Landing, then Nealsville, then Saginaw, and then LaPrairie. The village council quit meeting in 1911 and remained dormant until 1948.
	"LaPrairie Magnet" newspaper started publications; last issue was June 1891. This newspaper became the "Grand Rapids Magnet" in June 1891. It was discontinued in 1906.
	Itasca Lumber Company started construction of Itasca Railroad, sometimes called Bass Brook Railroad, from Cohasset north for about 18 miles. Because of difficulty in procuring needed right of way, rails were removed in 1897 and sent to Deer River.
	Duluth and Winnipeg Railroad reached Grand Rapids. It extended to Cohasset in 1892.
1891	**Itasca County organized March 7. It was composed of territory of present counties of Itasca and Koochiching. Village of Grand Rapids incorporated and made the temporary county seat. An election in 1892 made Grand Rapids the county seat permanently.**
	J.P. Simms filed plat of Itasca City; later called Deer River. School District No. 2 was authorized for LaPrairie in July. "La Prairie News" newspaper published in LaPrairie.
1892	Road built from south end of Mississippi bridge to Pokegama Lake, now known as Highway 169.
	First Itasca County Fair held at Grand Rapids on south side of the Mississippi River.
	First public library started in Grand Rapids.
	The Presbyterian Church is the first church in Grand Rapids.
1893	**First St. Joseph's Catholic church in Grand Rapids built; burned in 1910.**
1895	Iron Range and Trout Lake Townships organized.
	D. M. Gunn rebuilds the Pokegama Hotel; had the first electric lights in the county installed in it.
	"Grand Rapids Herald Review" newspaper published.
	Deer River township organized.
1895	Central School built in Grand Rapids.
1896	Itasca County courthouse construction was completed and occupied for first time.
	"The Itasca News" newspaper begins in Deer River. In 1924, it became the "The Deer River News".

First known picture of bridge across the Mississippi River in Grand Rapids

Re-built Pokegama Hotel

First Itasca County Fair

Itasca County Courthouse

TIMELINE

1897   Construction is started on the Minneapolis & Rainy River Railroad north from Deer River to Craig.

1898   St. Benedict's Hospital was established. Early patients were mostly lumberjacks who purchased hospital tickets for $12.00 per year. It was operated by the Sisters of St. Benedict. The hospital closed in 1912. Village of Deer River incorporated. At that time it had a depot, three hotels, three stores, several restaurants, and a schoolhouse. School District No. 3 formed (transferred to Koochiching County in 1906 when that county was formed). 1902 School District No.4 formed (transferred to Koochiching County in 1906 when that county was formed). 1905 School District No. 7 & School District No. 8 formed (transferred to Koochiching County in 1906 when that county was formed).

1900   Lake Jessie Township organized. Bertha Fuller is first high school graduate from Central School.

1901   Feeley Township organized. Village of Cohasset was incorporated. Local Indians translated Cohasset as "meeting of many waters" due to the many tributaries. Bass Brook Township organized. Power dam construction started and Itasca Paper Company built. First paper was produced in 1902.

1902   Ardenhurst, Bigfork, Nashwauk, Nore and Third River Townships organized. "Itasca County Independent" newspaper first published. Hawkins Mine in Nashwauk was the first iron ore mine in Itasca County. The mine ceased operations in 1962.

1903   New Grand Rapids High School ready for occupancy. Alvwood (formerly Island Lake), Moose Park, and Sago townships organized. King Lumber Company was founded in Grand Rapids. Eventually they had 9 lumber yards: Bovey, Calumet/Marble, Keewatin, Chisholm, Bigfork, Deer River, Warba, Remer, and Cass Lake. School District No. 9 organized in Nashwauk. Village of Nashwauk incorporated - first mining town in Itasca County. Incorporation set off a building boom. Population swelled from 220 in 1902 to 2,080 in 1920. "Bigfork Settler" newspaper in Bigfork begins publication.

1904   Goodland and Kinghurst (formerly Popple) Townships organized. A new plat filed by John C. Greenway for model village to be called Coleraine. Oliver Iron Mining Company erects 106 homes for rental. Village of Bovey incorporated. It was developed as a logging site in the mid 1880s and later became a mining town. School District No. 5 formed in Suomi & Jessie Lake area; rejoined School District No. 1 in 1935.

St. Benedict's Hospital

Itasca Paper Mill

Itasca Independent Office

King Lumber Company

John C. Greenway Cabin

1905	Grand Rapids Public Library, with a $10,000 Andrew Carnegie grant, is built. Grattan Township organized. Road built from Grand Rapids east to Bovey. Township of Marcell (formerly Big Turtle Lake) is organized. "The Itasca Iron News" newspaper, continuation of "The Bridgie News", "The News", and "The Northome News", located in Bovey. First ski jump and club house erected near Trout Lake in Coleraine. Gran Township (detached from Goodland Township) organized, later dissolved by 1910. School District No. 6 formed in Deer River area.
1906	School District No. 11 formed in Goodland; merged with School District No. 9 in the 1950s. Bearville and Carpenter Townships organized. Koochiching County separates from Itasca County. Construction of Greenway School in Coleraine begins and dedicated in 1907. Duluth Mesaba & Northern Railroad came to Coleraine. Village of Keewatin organized. Mining was the mainstay of Keewatin. Mines such as the St. Paul, Bray, Mississippi, Bennett and Mesabi Chief were located there. School District No. 9 formed in Nashwauk-Keewatin area. School District No. 10 formed in southwestern part of the county; included areas of Harthan, Leighton Brook, Rice Rapids, and White Oak. It rejoined School District No.1 in 1948.
1907	Village of Bigfork incorporated. Bigfork was created by loggers, fur traders and trappers. Its major business was logging done in the early 20th century. Arbo, Balsam and Wirt Townships organized. Road built between Grand Rapids and Deer River to the west. Village of Taconite incorporated. In its pre-1900 days it was named Holman. As mining pervaded the area, that settlement was absorbed by Taconite and was another of the planned villages sponsored by John C. Greenway. "The Coleraine Optic" newspaper begins in Coleraine.
1908	Good Hope, Greenway and Sand Lake Townships organized. President Theodore Roosevelt, under an act of Congress in 1908, created the Minnesota National Forest. In 1928 it became known as the Chippewa National Forest.
1909	Blackberry and Harris Townships organized. Village of Marble, a community built by Oliver Iron Mining Division of U. S. Steel to accommodate miners, was incorporated. It was named after R.N. Marble, a former U.S. Steel official. The village had a valuation of 5 ½ million dollars and was rated second richest in the world. It was first called "White City" because it was comprised entirely of tents in the midst of a dense forest. Village of Coleraine incorporated; population is 1481. Village of Calumet incorporated. In 1880, logging

Grand Rapids Library

Coleraine Ski Hill

Taconite Mining Drill

Village of Bigfork

TIMELINE

companies brought the first ettlers to the Calumet area. By 1909, businesses included a general store, hardware store, women's clothing store, blacksmith shop, cigar factory, ice house, livery barn, butcher shop, public sauna and fourteen saloons. Hill Annex Mine was the chief employer for many years. Deer River High School is built.

Marble

1910 Oteneagen and Wawina townships organized.

"The Eastern Itascan" newspaper began in Nashwauk.

1911 Spang Township organized.

Coleraine Public Library, with a $15,000 Andrew Carnegie donation, is built. Cost of library is $17,537.00.

Calumet

Village of Warba incorporated. Warba saw its boom years between 1905 and 1918. In this time they had a brick yard, sawmill, two hotels, a school and a bank. Warba was a town of wood sidewalks and dirt until 1925 when the highway was put through. It was first known as Verna.

Village of Zemple was incorporated. It was a busy lumber town with a sawmill, planing mill, box mill, veneer mill, a round-house, a boarding house and a population of more than 300 people. Located on the south end of Deer River, it became known as Deer River's "Industrial Suburb".

"The Deer River Times" newspaper was printed in Deer River.

1912 First "Bovey Farmers Day" was held.

1914 Longyear Park in Coleraine is developed.

Coleraine Public Library

"The Itasca Iron News" newspaper moves from Bovey to Coleraine.

1916 Bowstring (detached from Lake Jessie) Township organized.

St. Paul Dispatch and Pioneer Press newspapers purchased Itasca Paper Company for $600,000. Their business manager was C.K. Blandin who later purchased the mill and became its president.

1917 Lone Pine Township organized.

"Keewatin Chronicle" newspaper started in Keewatin, continuing "The Bigfork Settler" (Vol. 13) and "The Keewatin Plaintalk" (Vol. 3).

Warba

1918 Stokes (detached from Marcell) Township organized.

Itasca Hospital, with 30 beds, is built at a cost of $50,000. It was the first hospital in Minnesota to be constructed with county funds.

Charles Wilden poses for photographer Eric Enstrom and the world famous picture "GRACE" is born.

The last log drive down the Mississippi River.

1919 Morse (detached from Oteneagen) Township organized.

School District No.12 formed in Third River area; rejoined School District No. 1 in 1933.

1920 Lawrence (detached from Balsam) and Max Townships organized.

Original Black & White
GRACE Photograph

5

	Bridge is built over Pokegama Lake on road to Hill City.
1921	Wabana (detached from Balsam) Township organized.
	What might be the nation's only public school dormitory for high school students was built in Deer River and opened in 1921. This dormitory was built so that students who live far from the school would be able to attend school. They paid $25.00 a year and provided their own bedding. All housekeeping chores, except the cooking, were done by the girls and boys. The students went home on weekends. As many as 120 students lived there some years. The dormitory was in use until 1955, and was torn down in 1968.
	State Highway built from Grand Rapids east across the Range after a bitter fight.
	Daily bus service between Coleraine and Bigfork started.
	Village of Cooley incorporated; dissolved in 1974.
1922	Liberty (detached from Wirt) Township organized; was dissolved in 2015.
	New Greenway High School built in Coleraine.
	Keewatin High School completed.
1923	"The Bovey Press" newspaper in Bovey begins.
1924	"Itasca Farmer" newspaper first published in Coleraine. The newspaper was printed monthly for farmers. It ceased publication in 1931.
1925	Pomroy (detached from Wirt) Township organized.
	"The Bigfork Times" newspaper in Bigfork begins publication.
	School District No. 13 formed in Grave Lake area (separated from School District No. 5); united with School District No. 6 in 1933.
1927	Construction of Highway 38 from Grand Rapids north to Bigfork is completed.
1928	Bigfork High School completed.
1929	Name of paper mill changed to Blandin Paper Company. Coleraine airport was dedicated on July 4. Eight planes presented a program.
1932	Minneapolis & Rainy River railroad (Gut & Liver) abandons 63 miles of its lines. Streets in Grand Rapids renamed and numbered.
1933	Itasca County airport in Grand Rapids opens as a grass strip. Dedication in July 1935.
	The first of 15 Civilian Conservation Corps (CCC) camps were built in the county.
1936	Art Otis started his airport at Sugar Lake; dedication ceremonies took place in 1940.
1937	"The Itasca Progressive" newspaper was printed in Bigfork.

Last log drive

Bridge over Pokegama Lake

Blandin Paper Company

Coleraine Airport

TIMELINE

1938   Bigfork Hospital (Northern Itasca Hospital) constructed. Coleraine Hospital built.

1940   Dairyland Electric Cooperative, later known as Lake Country Power, formed for south central part of county; Northern Itasca Cooperative formed for northern part of county.
Village of Effie incorporated.
Village of Squaw lake incorporated.
Charles K. Blandin foundation established.

1941   New ski jump built at Mt. Itasca, west of Coleraine.
Grand Opening Blandin Foundation

1944   Sheriff's office apprehended 2 German prisoners who had escaped from the POW camp at Bena in Cass County.
Deer River Hospital established.

1948   ITASCA COUNTY HISTORICAL SOCIETY IS ESTABLISHED!

1949   Bigfork Airport constructed.
Philadelphia Eagles football team trains in Grand Rapids. In 1951, the Green Bay Packers football team trains here.

1950   "Pike For Vets" project started in Grand Rapids to provide a walleye dinner for patients at the VA Hospital in Minneapolis.

1956   Grand Rapids Showboat – "Mississippi Melodie" – started yearly performances that lasted for 60 years until 2015 when it disbanded.
North Star Stampede Rodeo was started on the North Star Ranch near Effie by Howard Pitzen.
Air Force Radar Base opens in Grand Rapids with 30 men. That number grew to 132 airmen and seven civilians by 1963 when it closed.

1957   Statewide renumbering of School Districts was implemented. School District No. 1 became No. 318; School District No. 2 became No. 316; School District No. 6 became No. 317; School District No. 9 became No. 319.

1958   Clay Boswell Unit 1 starts producing power; Unit 2 starts in 1960 and Unit 3 joined them in 1973. Unit 4 was completed in 1980.

1959   "The Western Itasca Review" newspaper was started in Deer River. This was a merger of the "Deer River News" and "The Itasca Progressive".

1960   "Scenic Range News" newspaper begins. This is a consolidation of "The Itasca Iron News" and "The Bovey Press".

1961   Marble Depot closed down.
Development began for the Sugar Hills Ski Area southwest of Grand Rapids.

1963   Itasca County and Minnesota became involved in Great River Road designation for routes along the Mississippi River.

Bigfork Hospital

Deer River Hospital

First Program

1965 The name of the Itasca Hospital changed to Itasca Memorial Hospital. It had grown from 30 to 108 beds, from 300 patients to 3,000, from 3 physicians to 35, from 4 employees to 320, from a $2,000 budget to $16,000,000.
Butler Taconite plant was built. Closed in the summer of 1985.

1967 National Steel Pellet at Keewatin sent out its first shipment of pellets.

Itasca Memorial Hospital

Itasca Junior College moves its campus from Coleraine to the North Central School and Experiment Station in Grand Rapids.

1974 All villages in Minnesota became known as cities.

1975 First Judy Garland Festival, organized by artist Jackie Dingmann. The festival has become a yearly event and is now known internationally. Many years, members of the Wizard of Oz cast have been in attendance.
Plans began to establish the Forest History Center located 1 ½ miles west of Grand Rapids on the Mississippi River and maintained by the Minnesota Historical Society.

1976 Skier Jim Maki of Coleraine competed in the Winter Olympics in Austria; he also competed in the Winter Olympics at Lake Placid in 1980.

1980 Grand Rapids man, Bill Baker, helps Team USA win gold in hockey in the Winter Olympics at Lake Placid, NY.

Original Poster

1985 Splithand Township organized.
Taconite Trail linking Ely to Grand Rapids opens. The trail includes 165 miles and took 14 years to complete.

1986 Sugar Brook Township organized, dissolved 4 months later.

1988 "Vinterslass" incorporated and held winter events in Grand Rapids.

1989 Wildwood Township is organized.
Itasca Memorial Hospital is expanded and the name is changed to Itasca Medical Center.
White Oak Fur Post built north of Deer River to depict early fur trading times.

1993 Funding received for construction of the Mesabi Range Trail (for biking and hiking). Mesabi Trail will traverse 145 miles and connect 28 communities from Grand Rapids to Ely. When completed, the trail will be one of the longest paved trails in the U.S.

Vinterslass Sculpture

1994 Highway 38 designated as Minnesota Scenic Byway and in 1996 it became the Edge of the Wilderness National Scenic Byway.

2003 "Scenic Range NewsForum" newspaper in Bovey starts publication, a continuation of the "Scenic Range News".

2005 Work on causeway over Pokegama Lake begins on Highway 169.
Grand Opening of new Grand Itasca Clinic/Hospital.

2010 Mary Shideler, the "Kayak Lady" completes her quest to paddle 1007 lakes in Itasca County over the past 15 years.

2013 Leech Lake Ojibwe Flag raised at the Itasca County Courthouse and Grand Rapids Area Chamber of Commerce.

2014 Grand Rapids State Bank celebrated its 100th birthday, the oldest locally owned bank in Itasca County.

Grand Rapids State Bank

2015 Dinosaur "claw" found at Hill-Annex mine; possibility of other fossils being explored.

MAPS

The following maps show the progression of the formation of Itasca County through January 2016.

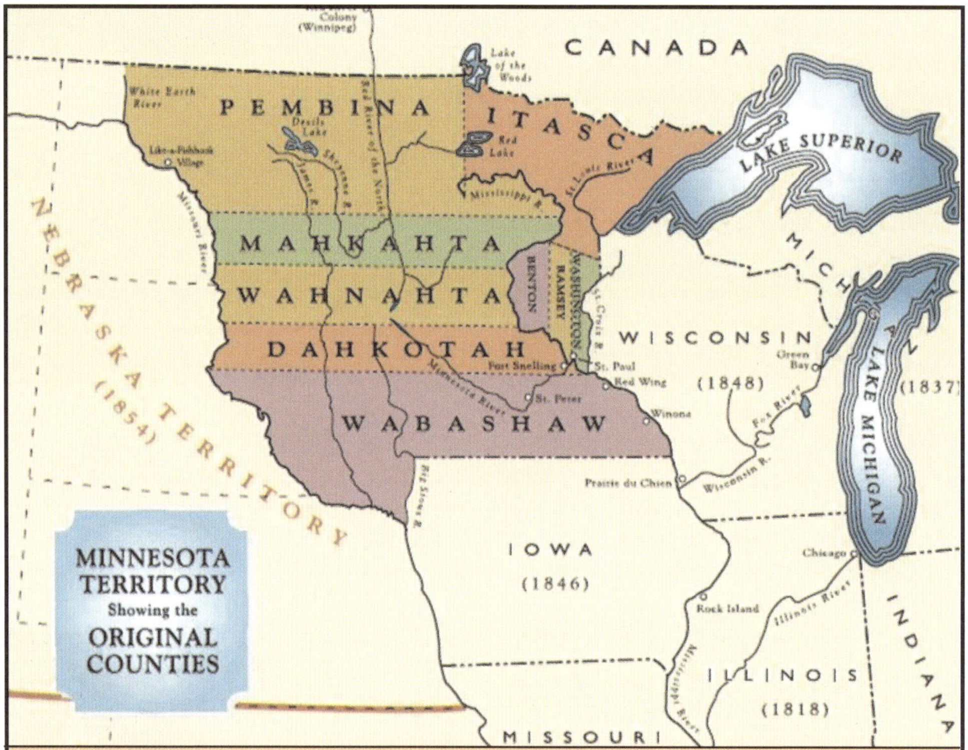

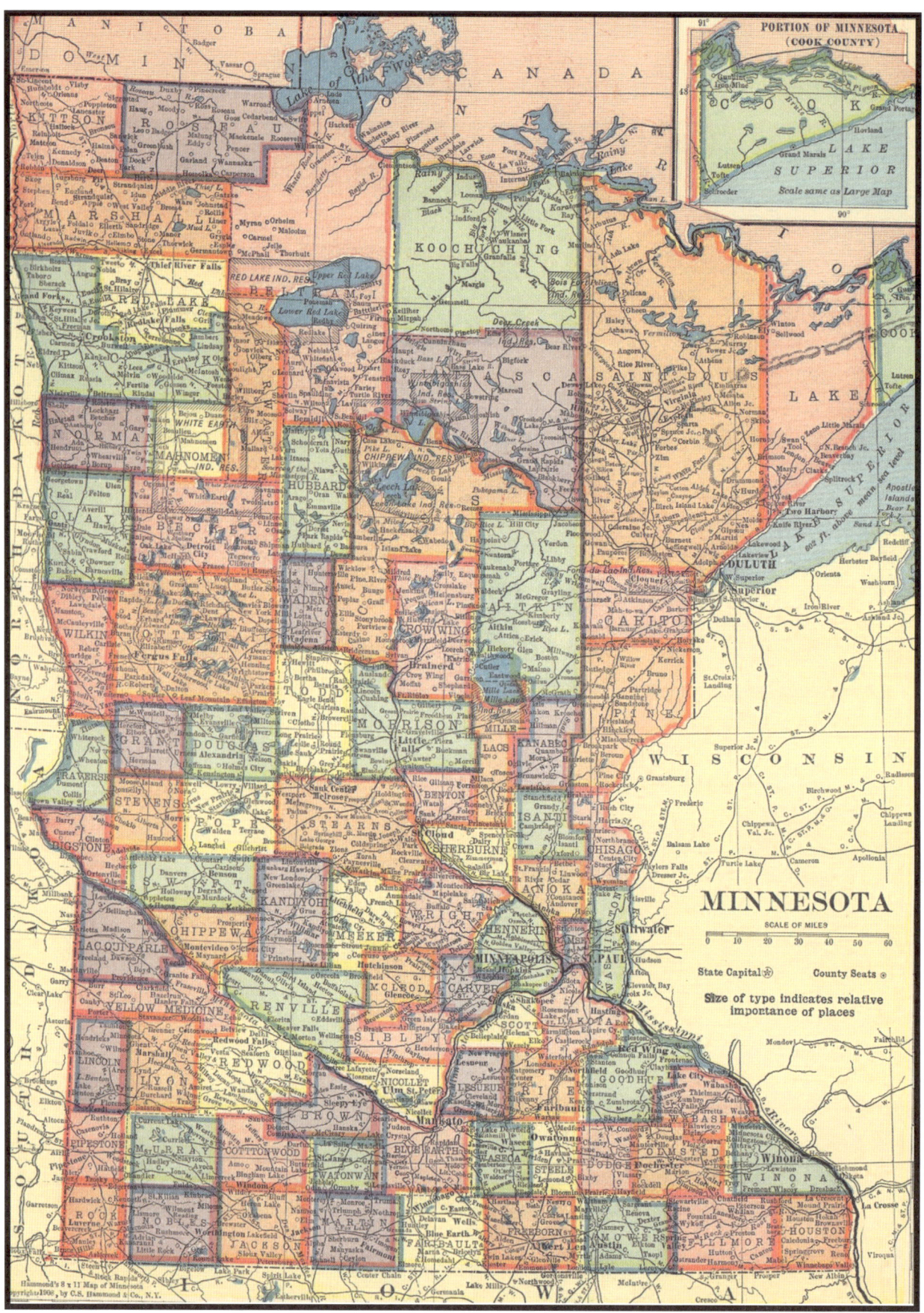

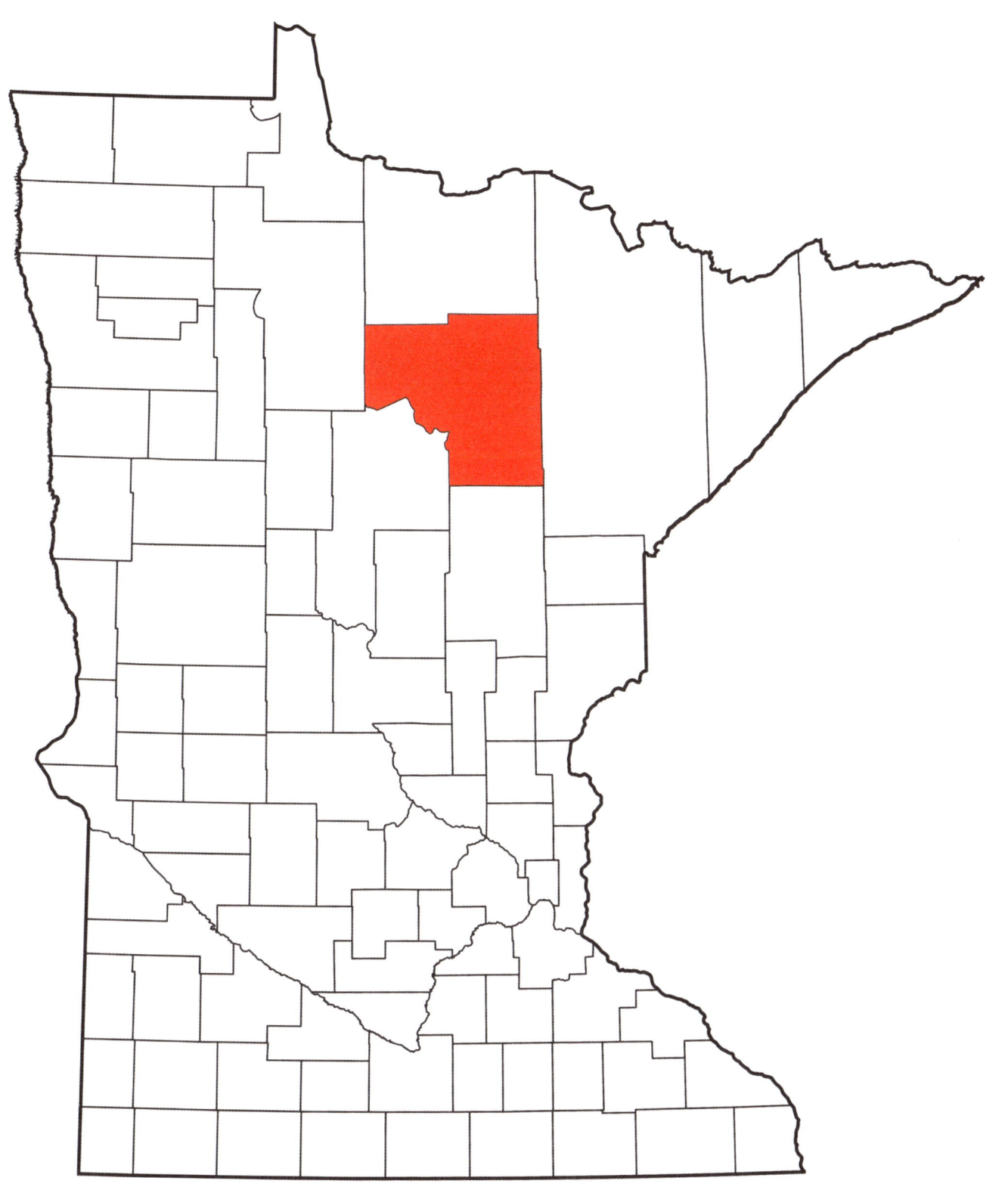

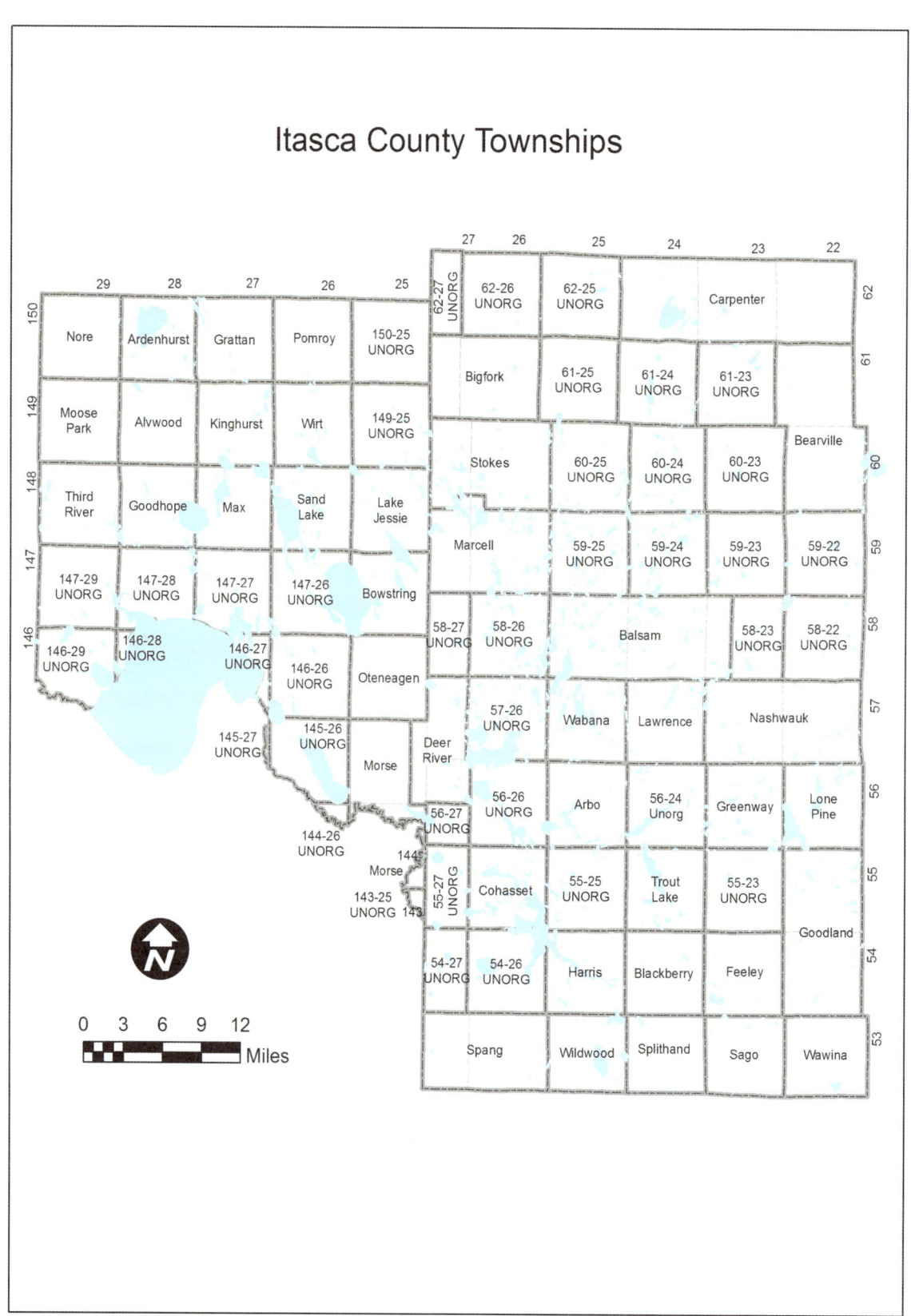

PREFACE

A quasquicentennial is a celebration of 125 years. That's the reason this book was written, to note that milestone for Itasca County. This is not, however, a definitive history. That would take an encyclopedia. This is meant to be an appetizer. Just a taste of what happened, where, and by whom.

The history of Itasca County runs through three centuries, from the late 1800s to the early 2000s.

The purpose of this book is to give you a glimpse of those people who mattered in the making of that history, as well as those who were made (or made up) by that history. To give the facts a face and give the legends a life.

Any potential culturally insensitive language from the period in which it was taken is included for historical purposes only.

Children from Polish Immigrants

Welcome House in front of Central School

Bovey Farmer's Day

Itasca County Fair

Town Stories

Itasca County

There was nothing simple or quick about becoming Itasca County. It took nearly two hundred years from the time the explorer La Salle took possession of the Mississippi Valley in 1682 in the name of Louis the Great of France until Itasca County was organized in 1891.

In between, Nicholas Perrot claimed the countries and rivers inhabited by the Sioux for France in 1689. The Northwest Territory was then created in 1787 followed by the Louisiana Purchase giving the United States title to Minnesota lying south and west of the Mississippi.

Finally, in 1849 the Minnesota Territory was established forming Itasca County which included parts of Aitkin and Cass Counties as well as Carlton, Lake, Cook, Koochiching, and St. Louis Counties.

One by one those counties detached and were organized separately. Itasca took its turn and became organized as the county it is today in 1891.

That is history. It was time for the people to start making it personal.

County Seat Feud

One of the most notorious feuds in county history resulted when it came time to select the county seat.

When Itasca County came into existence in 1891, LaPrairie had already been incorporated as a town; Grand Rapids had not. And there the feud begins.

Both locations desired the distinction of being the county seat and the economical bonus that goes with the title.

In 1891, the Minnesota Legislature authorized the organization of Itasca as a separate county which would have a three-man board who could choose a temporary county seat. What they did was create three county commissioner districts with those commissioners appointed by Minnesota Governor William Merriam. Those commissioners, Lafayette Knox, John P. Sims, and B. C. Finnegan, then designated Grand Rapids as the temporary county seat.

However, Senator William P. Allen was an influential figure in making recommendations to Governor Merriam. A. G. Bernard, editor and proprietor of the LaPrairie Magnet newspaper, met with Allen to lobby for one commissioner from LaPrairie to be appointed and for LaPrairie to be the county seat.

It appears that Bernard believed that Senator Allen had promised him the board of commissioners would include three representatives, one each from Grand Rapids, the Iron Range and LaPrairie. As it turned out, the senate and the governor selected two from Grand Rapids, one from the range and none from LaPrairie.

Feeling betrayed by Allen, Bernard wrote in his LaPrairie Magnet:

"When Judas Iscariot betrayed the Saviour he had the decency to go and hang himself. The people of LaPrairie have no reason to believe that Senator Allen has even so high an appreciation of the sense of honor, that he will go and do likewise…"

Grand Rapids was confirmed as county seat in the first regular county election in 1892.

Epidemics

Itasca County, though still remote in 1918, was not so isolated that the misery of the world could be avoided. At no time were Itascans immune to the epidemics that swept through history.

As late as the 1950s people of Itasca County and across the nation were being crippled or killed by polio. This virus attacks the spinal cord which leads to paralysis and often results in muscular atrophy with permanent deformities. The greatest horrors were that polio is highly contagious and that it has a penchant for affecting children.

Nurses went on home visits during the crisis

Polio epidemic reached its peak nationally in 1952 killing more than 3000 people. Four of those deaths occurred in Itasca County where more than fifty cases had been recorded. Because of its infectious nature, there were often multiple children within one family afflicted at the same time.

The iron lung was one tool implemented to combat the effects of the disease. This artificial respirator helped alleviate breathing difficulties sometimes suffered by polio patients. The equipment was costly so women of Itasca County stepped up to raise funds for securing the device and to aid in polio research. In late 1953 the women organized the "Mother's

Close quarters caused problems

March", a March of Dimes fund raising crusade. Combined with other contributions, more than $3500 was raised that year. It would be just two years before Dr. Jonas Salk developed a polio vaccine effectively eradicating the disease in the United States and other developed nations. The women of Itasca County played a role in that successful medical action.

Certainly vaccines were not a new creation. They had been developed and effective for decades. Such is the case of the small pox vaccine. Developed by Edward Jenner in the year 1798, a small pox vaccination would prevent a person from contracting the disease. Small pox is easily transmitted where personal hygiene or sanitation is ignored. The close confines of north woods logging camps in Itasca County of the 1850s made the small pox epidemic almost inevitable.

Drinking water came from wells situated too close to camp latrines or which held drainage from manure piles. Add to that winter months when breaking through ice made it a real chore to wash anything and you have a roiling cauldron of infection. It only took the transient nature of loggers and lumberjacks to initiate an epidemic.

So it happened in late 1882 that reports came of small pox at the Caldwell logging camp located northwest of Bigfork. Shortly, small pox claimed the life of a logger in Grand Rapids.

It would not end there. Small pox did not discriminate in its assault on humanity. In fact, it would seem that in his campaign to efface the Indian nation, the white man might have done it as easily with a kiss as with a bullet. The Ojibwe of Itasca County had no immunities with which to combat either the mundane or the malicious diseases of European settlers.

The proximity of logging camps to Chippewa reservations and the interactions of loggers and the Ojibwe created an opening for the spread of small pox to the Indigenous People with devastating results.

Dairyland Electric

Things were not completely bleak, however. In the ensuing years communities established hospitals and schools were built throughout the county. Roads were constructed linking Grand Rapids to rural communities and yet, as late as 1940, rural Itasca County had yet to enjoy the luxury of electricity. In point of fact, at that time only around 10% of U.S. farmers were served by central station electricity. Keep in mind that just twenty years later Alan Shepard, Jr. would be the first American in space.

It was time for civilization to light up the rural landscape, but for Itasca County, that wouldn't come easily.

In 1940 approximately 1000 people attended a meeting at Grand Rapids City Hall organized by Itasca County Extension Agent, A. H. Frick. The purpose was to organize an electric cooperative. Many of the

Power Lines

attendees had heard of the incredible advantages rural farmers had received with the advent of electricity. Farmers contributed to the new Dairyland Electric Cooperative and took on the task of clearing power line right-of-ways.

George Taus was hired to supervise the work in Dairyland's area. He barely began his efforts when he fell ill and died.

The General Engineering Corporation then took over the work, sending Henry Dahl as the resident engineer. But just three days after his arrival in Grand Rapids, Dahl was killed in an auto accident. Bleak as that made the prospect of completion, troubles had only begun.

Easements now had to be secured from property owners when laws forbid the purchasing of right-of-ways.

On top of all that, not all local residents were readily willing to give way to the expansion of modernization. Some were just plain obstinate. Others felt they were threatened - by whom is not clear - to allow access to their land.

Whatever the obstacles, the first Rural Electric Association (REA) pole was set in October 1940 and by January of 1941 rural Itasca County had electricity available to them.

Ku Klux Klan

It is perhaps human nature to diminish those portions of history which don't speak well of ourselves. That may be why not much is said about the presence of the Ku Klux Klan (KKK) in Itasca County. There is one recorded account of a gathering of the group in 1925 at the Itasca County Fairgrounds.

Even though a cross burning had been documented in Bovey the year before, county commissioners agreed to lease the county fairgrounds to the KKK.

The Klan, with their extreme philosophy of hatred and contempt for Jews, African-Americans, Roman Catholics, and a host of others, was organized in the deep South of the United States in 1867. It virtually disappeared with just a few local claverns active until the 1920s when the resurgence of proponents for more equitable treatment of all segments of the population began.

At that point, Klan activities infiltrated regions of the nation far from the South. And so, in 1925, the Klan came to Itasca County.

Having leased the fairgrounds they commenced with a program that started with a parade of hundreds of Klan members in their notable white robes. The parade led to the grandstand where the speaker regaled the crowd with the positions and philosophy of the Klan.

The local newspaper seemed to be ambiguous in their coverage since they never mentioned the Klan's terroristic history, their religious bigotry, or racism. Rather, they commended the organization's impressive fireworks display and how well they cleaned up the site after the gathering. They reported that up to 8000 people attended the Ku Klux Klan rally.

It would seem curiosity played more of a role than interest in being recruited that attracted such a large turnout since little is heard of Klan activities in Itasca County beyond this event.

KU KLUX KLAN
OPEN AIR ENTERTAINMENT
GRAND RAPIDS
North End of Village
PUBLIC INVITED
Magnificent Display of Klan
FIREWORKS
NATIONAL SPEAKER
SATURDAY, OCTOBER 3rd
PROGRAM STARTS 7:30 P. M.
LUNCH AND REFRESHMENTS   ADMISSION FREE

LaPRAIRIE

When great stands of timber were found in Itasca County, it didn't seem to matter whether or not there was an established community nearby.

Treaties with the Ojibwe in1854-55 opened up logging on the Upper Mississippi River which meant the banks of the Prairie River could now be accessed.

Other areas in Minnesota, like the St. Croix Valley, had been conducting significant logging operations since the 1830s. But the far north tributaries of the Mississippi River grew white pine that rivaled those areas. So in the early 1870s, cutting began.

Wes Day built a "brush warehouse" where the Prairie River meets the Mississippi. That was also the location of Neal Carr's Landing, or Nealsville, for steamboats.

Along with early settlers Day and Carr, John G. Fraser came to LaPrairie in 1886 with his bride, the former Grace Arbo, whose family gave their name to Arbo Township.

Fraser would be a prominent resident, beginning as a log driver, then operating LaPrairie's first hotel (Fraser House), as a trustee of the 1891 city incorporation council, as a School District #2 board member, and as one of the first to hold a liquor license.

LaPrairie was on its way to being the hub of Itasca County when it incorporated in 1890. It beat Grand Rapids on that account. But it also had the first hospital, bank and newspaper in the county. All of that wouldn't be enough to make LaPrairie the county seat.

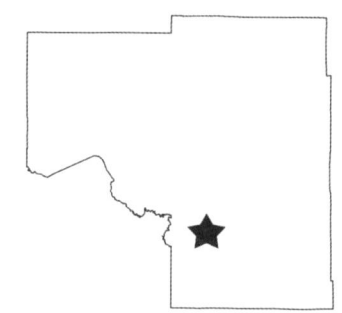

Steamboat Houghton
in LaPrairie

Hotel Fraser in background

Original LaPrairie Town Hall

GRAND RAPIDS

The difficulty with including the words "Grand Rapids" in a compilation of stories regarding Itasca County is that it conjures up different images for different people.

Do you automatically think of tourism? Is your first thought a site for culture in Northern Minnesota? Or is it a recreation area with swimming, boating, and fishing lakes right in the city limits? Is Grand Rapids a retirement community or a magnet for families?

Perhaps the quickest way to define Grand Rapids is by the numbers.

Grand Rapids, the village, was incorporated in 1891 and established as the county seat of Itasca County in 1892.

Before that, the Potter Company general store became the first permanent building in 1872. Duluth & Winnipeg Railroad station was built in 1890.

Bridge into downtown Grand Rapids

It was critical that travel from the Mississippi River bridge to Pokegama Lake be simplified and to that end, a road was built in 1891 connecting the two.

Within three years of incorporation Grand Rapids had a municipal water system, telephones, and electric lights.

Unknowingly, residents of Grand Rapids built historical sites, including Central School in 1895, which would be treasured into the 21st century.

4th of July Parade

Panorama view of 4th street

22

Folks in Grand Rapids may have been unaware of the diverse value of the trees in the area until 1901 with the formation of Itasca Paper Company and its startup of a paper mill which would one day be known as Blandin Paper Company.

Pokegama Avenue looking North

Grand Rapids Area Chamber of Commerce

Celebrating Golden Anniversary in 1941

Who better to tell the story of the Blandin Paper Company than its owner? Among the many transcripts left by Charles K. Blandin, the following piece was found in the Blandin Paper Company public relations office. This history was written by Blandin and dated July 19, 1946. It is reprinted here exactly as it was found.

History of Blandin Paper Company

It has often been said that the progress, the greatness, or the welfare of a community, a nation, or even of a business flows from the dreams or the visions of the men and women who guide its destinies. I believe it can be truly said that progress in any field depends on men and women of vision who have the courage and the daring to put visions and ideas into tangible or usable form. They must not only have the dreams, they must also have the ability and the stamina to make them come true.

It was because there were such men in Grand Rapids a half century ago that a paper mill was built.

On January 6, 1899, seven of these men met to organize a corporation to be named the Grand Rapids Water Power & Boom Company. The seven incorporators were Dan Gunn, Hubert Powers, LaFayette Knox, Dan Doran, George Meyers, John Costello and John Beckfelt. Their purpose in organizing was to begin the development of the water power of the Mississippi at Grand Rapids and to find an industrial use for the power which would create employment for the people of the community.

C. K. Blandin

They believed there was sufficient timber to justify the building of a pulp and paper mill, and they set out to find capital and management for that purpose.

Among those interested was Mr. Boyce, Publisher of the SATURDAY BLADE in Illinois. Mr. Boyce employed timber cruisers to determine whether there were enough trees for pulpwood to warrant the building of a mill. He decided there weren't and lost interest. (Since then the mill has ground more than a million cords of wood into pulp, and we now use between twenty-five and thirty thousand cords every year.)

About this same time a group from Kaukana, Wisconsin, was interested in building a paper mill, and on August 6, 1900, Mr. A. C. Bossard of that group attended a meeting of the Board of Directors to discuss the matter. Following this, a mutually satisfactory proposal was developed and it was accepted by the Directors on November 30, 1900.

The original incorporators had thus accomplished their task. A paper mill for Grand Rapids was assured, and December 10, 1900, all of them resigned as officers and directors in favor of the Kaukana, Wisconsin, group, which consisted of Frank F. Becker, A. C. Bossard, L. Lindauer and Henry G. Becker.

Construction was soon started and the mill was completed early in 1902, at a total cost approximating $230,000. The first paper from the new mill was billed to the General Paper Company of Milwaukee, Wisconsin, on March 8, 1902, and in dollars amounted to $639.96.

During the construction period, or to be exact on July 1,1901, the new owners organized the Itasca Paper Company to take over the mill upon completion. This corporation is still in existence and is now known as Blandin Paper Company, the name having been changed in 1928.

From the beginning in 1902, the new mill produced newsprint at the rate of about 25 tons per day. It continued at about that rate until and through 1916.

This was during World War I and circulation and size of metropolitan dailies was growing by leaps and bounds. As publisher of the ST.PAUL DISPATCH and PIONEER PRESS, I could see the danger to our papers unless we could assure ourselves of a supply of print paper. This was no vision and no dream, but a stern reality. The shortage of newsprint was becoming more acute by the day. I set out, therefore, to make sure of our paper supply. I was willing to buy a paper mill if that was necessary to obtain paper. I learned that the Grand Rapids mill might be bought at a price. The principal stockholder was Frank Becker, who lived in Kaukana, Wisconsin. I journeyed there and after a brief talk our newspapers became the owner of the Grand Rapids mill.

After fifteen years of operation, it wasn't much of a mill anymore, but it could still produce paper. By making improvements and by increasing the speed of the machine, we soon increased production to between 40 and 50 tons per day, as against the 25 or 30 it had been making.

After the war ended in 1918 the paper shortage continued, and in 1922-23 we installed a second machine bringing production to 75 tons per day, all of which was still being consumed in the publication of the St. Paul papers.

In 1927 I sold the newspapers but retained the paper mill, and there arose the problem of what to do to continue the mill as a business that could stand on its own feet. It is true we had a long-term contract to supply the St. Paul papers and the production of newsprint was still profitable. The prices of news, however, was in a definite downtrend, and the overproduction caused by the large-scale Canadian building of news mills during the twenties almost assured eventual operating losses. To make the matter worse, our small machines had to compete with many large, new high-speed Canadian machines, and if it came to a time when these operated at a loss, conditions might be disastrous for the small mills with small and slow-speed machines.

To survive, it seemed to me we would have to modernize and increase the output in order to bring the cost of production as nearly as possible into line with the lowest cost producers in the industry. We planned our program accordingly. We obtained a long-term contract under which we sold the additional production to be made and then proceeded to build new facilities and improve the old.

We rebuilt the building into the first windowless paper mill in the world, and we installed a large, modern machine having a rated speed of 1,500 feet per minute and capable of producing 100 tons of paper per day. The small machine installed in 1923 was eliminated through sale, and the original machine was further improved. Where necessary, auxiliary equipment was improved or added. To take care of the increased power requirements, we added a high pressure boiler and turbo generator capable of producing 4,000 K.W. of electricity.

We now had what we believe was one of the most modern newsprint mills in the world. The wisdom of having made it so was proven as the future unfolded. During the early 1930's when 75% of the North American newsprint production was in receivership we were able to operate at or above the black line.

While this was an accomplishment, it was not enough. To insure survival and continued progress a business must earn a fair return on the capital invested to carry on the business. This had not been possible in the production of newsprint, and I came to the definite conclusion that the future of the mill would be much more assured by the production of other grades of paper. In 1935 we began producing groundwood specialty papers on a small scale. Over the years the tonnage of those grades was increased until now we have eliminated newsprint altogether.

The production of these other grades required greater care in grinding the wood, and more refining, mixing, etc. Briefly, it required more power. Also, some of the other equipment in the power plant was becoming obsolete, and in 1941 we remedied this situation by installation of another boiler and generator unit capable of producing an additional 4,000 K.W. of electricity.

Groundwood specialty papers cover a wide range of grades, but they can be divided into two kinds of basic usages, that is, for magazine printing and for converting. During the last few years we decided to specialize on the production of magazine papers, and at the present time a substantial portion of our tonnage is being sold for such magazines as "Look", "Successful Farming", "Better Homes and Gardens", and others.

This, again, required improvements, and we are now engaged in a large scale improvement program which will permit controlled quality and reduce the cost of production, which gives us further assurance of progress and of maintaining or improving our position in the industry.

At the outset, I mentioned the names of seven men who were responsible for the building of a paper mill in Grand Rapids. To many of you these are just names, but those who live in Grand Rapids recognize in these names fellow citizens of the community - relatives of those seven men, and because the paper mill survived and progressed, they, with others, benefit from the vision and the foresight of their forebears.

This brings me to another phase. These men were unselfish in building for the future welfare of the community, and now, as always, there are other opportunities to follow their example. In recent years we have heard more and more about the conservation of our forests; we have been urged to "KEEP MINNESOTA GREEN" and to grow more trees. We are going to hear more of this in the future because of the importance of trees to Minnesota. The Forest Industries Information Committee recently released an estimate which values the forest products harvested in Minnesota in 1945 at $90,956,000.00, without setting up anything for recreational value.

To protect our forests or to plant trees which need fifty or more years to mature requires the vision and the unselfishness exemplified by the seven men I have mentioned, but it may well be that such action by us today will insure an industry for Grand Rapids in the next half century.

When I bought the mill, and for a time after, it was my intention to dispose of it after the paper shortage had been cured, but the more I came to Grands [sic] the better I liked the community and its people. I began to dream, and I had visions of a paper mill that was different. I began to have visions of a factory my neighbors would be proud of instead of merely tolerating because it provided income to the community. Throughout the years, those thoughts and that vision were an important factor in decisions to improve and build. My ambition has been and will be to give Grand Rapids more than the visions and the imagination of those seven men could see or believe possible.

Local delivery from the mill

Blandin Paper Company, the windowless mill.

This was the mill when C.K. Blandin arrived into town. Itasca Paper Mill

Katherine Lent

Not all the business visionaries in Grand Rapids were men and any list of "firsts" referring to Grand Rapids has to include Katherine Lent. Other women may have come to the area before Lent, but she was the first who came (1882) and stayed.

As with many explorers and settlers who ended up in remote, wilderness areas, as Grand Rapids was in the 1880s, it may have been an escape from a secret past life that brought Katherine Lent to Grand Rapids.

Emigrating from Ireland in 1849, Lent's parents, John and Merry Higgins, set sail to America. It was during this trip that Lent was born in the middle of the Atlantic Ocean.

The Higgins family moved about the eastern part of the country, eventually landing in Lake City, Minnesota. From there, Katherine moved with her husband Benjamin Lent to Ashtabula, Ohio, where she delivered two daughters. And this is where the secret life of Katherine Lent begins.

Only known picture of Katherine Lent, farthest right

The children were very young when Katherine left Ohio and located in Lake City. It was there that the Lent daughters were left with nuns in an orphanage as Katherine made her way to Grand Rapids on a steamboat. Once she had a stable life in Grand Rapids she sent for her girls Prelie and first born, Nellie.

They thrived in the near wilderness because Katherine was not only the first woman settler; she was the first businesswoman in Grand Rapids. Her business savvy served her well.

In time, Katherine conducted a hotel, owned a millinery shop where she designed and made hats, and had a funeral parlor. She eventually owned the equivalent of a city block, leasing store fronts to area businessmen.

She had gained respect as an entrepreneur and grand lady from lumberjacks, businessmen, and residents. That respect was perhaps the motivator in keeping her secret. For, although she had always told everyone that she was a widow, her descendants finally revealed her secret generations later.

Lent Millinery Shop

As told by her great granddaughter… "we, her great grandchildren, learned from her husband's military papers that she was, in fact, divorced. Being a young woman and a Catholic, she never would have gotten the respect that she did if her terrible secret had been revealed."

The respect she earned may also have become a legacy for her children as daughter, Nellie, continued in the tradition of "firsts". Nellie was Katherine's first born and in 1894 she married Mike Toole - the first elected sheriff of Itasca County.

Potato Festival

Sometimes the thing a community celebrates says a lot about a special moment they have experienced. The Grand Rapids Potato Festival is testimony to the importance agriculture once held for the town and surrounding areas.

Of the Potato Festivals celebrated 1939 to 1959, the 1951 event was surely the most notable. Cartoonist Al Capp, the Charles Schultz of his day, participated. He was not only the creator of the Li'l Abner cartoon series, but he designed the label for the Arrowhead Cannery. The cannery dealt, not with potatoes, but rutabagas, which explains the title of the 1951 Potato Festival—"Turnip & Tater Time".

It was said that folks out East didn't even believe rutabagas existed and insisted they were just yellow turnips. So it was that Capp's design for Arrowhead Cannery read "Li'l Abner Preserved Yellow Turnip".

It's believed 10,000-15,000 people viewed the Potato Festival parade that Saturday in September.

There was a children's parade which took nearly an hour and a half to pass. Children were awarded prizes in categories like "best wagon" and "best doll buggy". Ruth Ann Buckley was crowned Miss Grand Rapids. Awards for produce-growing skills went to "veteran potato grower from Pokegama Lake" Linter Underwood who won the governor's cup. Erwin Bertram took home the prize for largest rutabaga. A notable festival, indeed.

Crowds on 1st Avenue NW for Potato Festival

28

Other Notables

People in Grand Rapids were good at celebrating when fame came to Grand Rapids, a couple of times, in the form of youngsters.

Judy Garland, born Frances Ethel Gumm, came into the world at Itasca Hospital in 1922.

At the age of two she was performing with her sisters, Mary Jane and Virginia. Her father owned the Grand Theater on Pokegama Avenue where Garland performed her first solo, "Jingle Bells".

Undoubtedly best known for the 1939 movie, "Wizard of Oz", she lived in Grand Rapids just four short years. Her family moved to Los Angeles when she was four.

The world would hear about Grand Rapids again in 1980.

Bill Baker had played hockey for the Grand Rapids High School team and was playing at the University of Minnesota when he joined other young men from colleges across the country to form the U.S. Olympic Hockey Team in 1980. Their coach, Herb Brooks, would lead Baker and the others to the "Miracle on Ice" - which was not the gold-medal game as many believe. Instead, it was the game before the final against the Soviets. The world believed that the United States team had little or no chance at victory, but they defeated the Soviet team, 4-3. Following that, they beat Finland to take the gold medal.

The 1980 U. S. hockey team's performance has been referred to as "The Miracle on Ice".

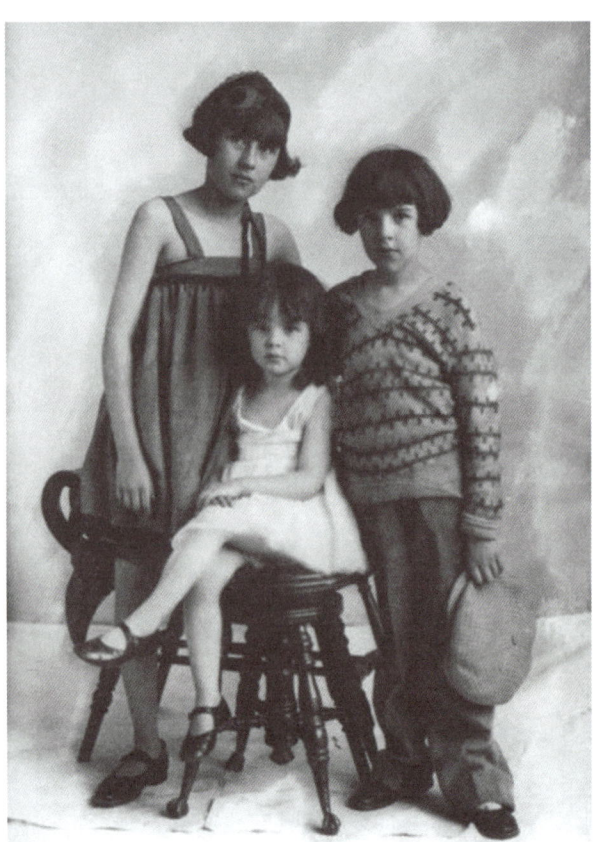

Photographer Eric Enstrom's picture of the Gumm sisters; Mary Jane, Virginia, and Frances Ethel

Bill Baker on 1980 U.S. Olympic Hockey Team

COHASSET

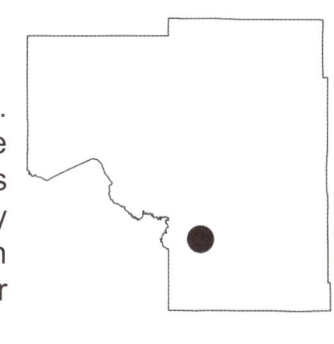

The original plat of Cohasset was done in early 1893. Cohasset then incorporated as a city in 1902. There is some dispute about the meaning of the word "Cohasset". Indians from Drumbeater Point say the name means "Meeting of many Waters", but Minnesota Historians, although agreeing it is an Indian name apropos, says it means "Place of Pines". Either was a fitting name for the village at the time of its founding.

Many lumber mills were quickly established as the little settlement grew. The Mississippi River and Bass Brook converge right there making logging enterprises very effective. Settlers also made use of the waterways and the six steamboats that once operated at Cohasset.

Great Northern Railway ran east and west through Cohasset giving the community even greater access for their timber products.

Cohasset Main Street

Acknowledged as the first settler in Cohasset, Sam Lawrence came to the area in 1892. His daughter, Jessie, established a homestead as well and it was her home that became the first school in 1894.

Businesses sprang up, including a post office in 1892, to serve the settlers and the logging companies. At one time both the Bass Brook Hotel and the St. Pierre served the community along with a photo gallery, restaurant, and sweet shop.

In the early 1900s there was another influx of settlers and many new businesses started. The largest of these enterprises was the Cohasset Hardwood Manufacturing Co. which was incorporated September 6, 1907. Directors of the company were E.L. Buck, Julius Rosholt, G.G. Wood, W.L. Wood, and H.S. Thompson. This company planned to use the large birch forest in the vicinity to manufacture butter pails and other small wares which required a good grade of hard wood.

Original Pail

Hardwood Manufacturing Company

Wood yard for the pail company

The factory ran 24 hours a day and provided work for many people.

A keeper of Cohasset history, lifelong resident Bud Payment told of his father coming to Cohasset in the early 1900s to work at the Cohasset Hardwood Manufacturing Company. Located between the river and the railroad, the pail factory manufactured large barrels, washtubs, candy pails and buckets for butter. The pail factory was Cohasset's largest employer until the mid 1920s when it burned. After the fire, many of the factory's workers, including Bud's father, went to Hill City where there was another pail factory.

Electricity was becoming more a necessity than a luxury across the nation and the state of Minnesota was no exception.

A number of small utility companies incorporated as Duluth Edison Electric Company in 1906. Then, consolidating many regional utilities, the company became Minnesota Power and Light Company in 1923. Power plants were built including the coal-fired Clay Boswell generating facility in Cohasset by 1958.

Minnesota Power and Light in 1959

An interesting part of Cohasset's history is its occasional identity crisis.

Bass Brook Township existed until 1991 when it became the city of Bass Brook. Cohasset separated from the township in 1916, but in 1957 a vote was taken to become one government. However, in 1975 that merger was dissolved. The township and city were sharing the responsibility of providing services but city residents found they could no longer afford a separate government. In 1994 the name of Bass Brook was gone and it was all called Cohasset. It is now governed by the Cohasset City Council which has a mayor as its leader.

Minnesota Power

TROUT LAKE TOWNSHIP

A quick glance at a plat map will tell you how Trout Lake Township got its name. Trout Lake, and others, cover more than four square miles of the township. And the lake itself garnered its name from the incredible numbers of lake trout held within it. The lake can reach depths of over one hundred feet. Trout Lake is translated from the Ojibwe word "*Namegoss*".

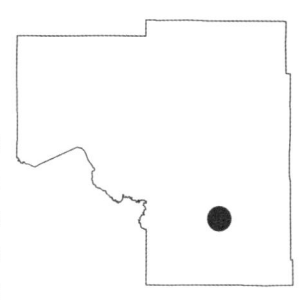

South of what is now Coleraine, Trout Lake featured fertile soil thought to be ideal for farming. Some of the early Finnish settlers made good on that promise.

Organized in 1894, Trout Lake Township is one of the oldest in Itasca County. It once neighbored Gran Township which had detached from Goodland Township in 1905. But Gran was not to enjoy a long life and within five short years had reverted to "unorganized township 55-23". By 1910 it was known merely as "Gran Precinct", a polling place for the 1910 election.

The schools of the area didn't fare much better. The Kjostad School, serving just two families, ran in 1919. There was a Gran School in 1915 built by School District #1. The Gran Consolidated School came along in 1922 but closed in 1932 and the students were sent to Trout Lake School.

That, too, is part of the past.

The wooded shorelines still attract people to the area. And fishing is still a favorite activity on the lake that gave its name to an entire township.

Brother and sister, Waino & Marie Karjala, were milk farmers. They supported many community projects, including the Itasca County Historical Society.

Marie Karjala doing milk chores.

DEER RIVER

The Deer River area must have looked like a forest of wealth to the early lumbermen arriving in the late 1800s.

Fur traders had enjoyed the bounty of the area since the 1860s and missionaries were working with the Ojibwe community about the same time. It is said that one missionary, Father Buh, serving on the White Oak Reservation, started the first school in Itasca County about 1869.

Known early on as "Itasca City", Deer River would become the logging center of western Itasca County. The Akeley Lumber Company was the first logging enterprise and was sold to Itasca Lumber Company around 1896. It wouldn't end there. Soon McAvity & Hurd, Voights, Hedquists, and Charles Seelye logging operations would thrive in Deer River.

By the time the village was incorporated in 1898, there was an active community of settlers creating businesses.

The railroads were making it possible for folks to establish a bank, hotels, a newspaper office, and stores offering hardware, clothing, and more.

Duluth & Winnipeg Railway (later absorbed by the Great Northern) formed a junction with the Minneapolis & Rainy River Railroad at Deer River.

Those railroads were advantageous, not only for the logging companies, but for all the mills being created. That was especially true for the small suburb of Deer River known as Mill Town. It was so called because of the large number of residents employed by the Joyce sawmill and planing mill, Bahr Brothers veneer mill, and the box mill owned by Rathburn, Hair & Ridgeway Company.

Deer River Train Depot

Deer River Street Scene

Naturally, there was a bit of a problem. Deer River Lumber Company had a mill and lumberyard located in Oteneagen Township. The residents there felt that those properties were undervalued and that they should be paying additional taxes. The Itasca Lumber Company, which had absorbed Deer River Lumber Company, challenged the way Oteneagen organized. That gave them enough time to petition for the incorporation of the village of Zemple (Mill Town) which could, in turn, separate from Oteneagen Township.

Deer River Recreation gas launch

It worked and in 1911 Zemple was incorporated as a village retaining the railroad yards, mill, machine shop, round house, and mill yard. Deer River kept the Minneapolis & Rainy River Railroad (M&RRR) depot.

The M&RRR pulled up in 1932 but some of the original Itasca Lumber Company homes remain in Zemple.

The largest landowner, R.T. Zempel, lent his name to the new town, even though the name was misspelled---and continues to be.

1897 Deer River school

With so much activity and so many families coming to the area, it was time to think about schools.

The people in Deer River and surrounding country side began with a log school that operated from 1894 to 1899. A new four-room frame school would be built just a year after county commissioners recognized School District #6 serving the Deer River area.

The size of District #6 was a problem. There were students who lived more than 50 miles from Deer River making it difficult to attend high school. Even with state aid, busing costs were prohibitive. The school board came up with an ingenious solution in 1921 with the addition of a dormitory to the school.

Likely the only high school dormitory in the United States, the "Dorm" operated from 1921 until 1955. It would cost each student $10 a year (bumped to $25 annually in 1951) and a little elbow grease.

Students were expected to wash dishes, help prepare meals, and clean up the dorm as well as their own rooms.

As special and unique as the "Dorm" was, the dormitory was demolished in 1968.

Earl Cooley homestead in 1907, NW of Deer River

IRON RANGE

There are times when history just won't stand still long enough to be written about. That is the case in the story of Iron Range Township which was only wiped off the map in 2014. Before that it was one of the oldest townships in Itasca County being organized in 1894.

Early maps help explain the name of the former township as some of the property holders listed included:

Hanna Mining
U.S. Steel Corporation
Balkan Mining
Cleveland Cliffs Iron Company
Genoa Iron Mining Company
Orwell Iron Company
Great Northern Iron Ore Properties
Jackson Iron Mining Company
Canisteo Mining Company
Mesaba Cliffs Iron Mining
Homestead Iron Mining Company
Syracuse Mining Company.

Man standing by horse was a diamond setter for the mines

The towns of Bovey, then Coleraine, Taconite, and Holman were in Iron Range Township. Now they're not, because Iron Range Township isn't there. It's been annexed to the town of Taconite.

Canisteo Mine Camp

Mining equipment

35

COLERAINE

Plans for the town of Washburn were drawn in 1904 but were dissolved when United States Steel purchased land near Trout Lake in 1906 and then filed a new plat for a model community. The Oliver Iron Mining Company (OIMC), a subsidiary of United States Steel Corporation, and its personnel played a critical role in the development of the town of Coleraine.

The village of Coleraine was incorporated in 1909. Meaning "Cole's Ridge", Coleraine was named for Thomas Cole, first president of OIMC, by its District Superintendent John C. Greenway

The original survey and design of a planned village is credited to Greenway. His vision was to create a model town with the aim of attracting the finest people. So important was this premise to Greenway that people needed to produce references before they were allowed to purchase town lots.

Greenway was also influential enough to approach philanthropist and multi-millionaire, Andrew Carnegie, for funds to construct a public library. Influential enough to receive from Carnegie $15,000 of the total $17,537 building cost. The library was placed in the National Register of Historic Places in 1979.

Greenway can also be credited - at least peripherally - with the development of Coleraine's ski jumping Olympic dynasties.

Once established, the ski club nurtured global competitors like Gene Wilson. Wilson (who, incidentally, was a technician with U.S. Steel in Coleraine) trained under Ole Mangseth, known as the "Father of Ski Jumping", in the 1920s and became a member of the 1940 U.S. Olympic Ski Jumping Team. Hopes of competing on the Olympic world stage were thwarted with the advent of World War II.

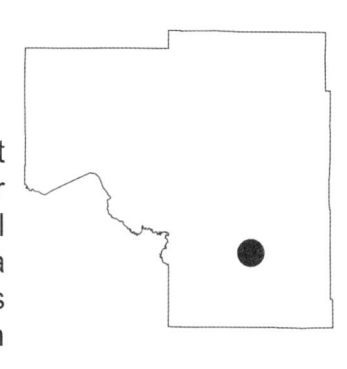

John C. Greenway (r) and H.C. Dudley in 1906 at Canisteo Mine entrance

Coleraine Street Grading

Saporro, Japan was to host the winter games in 1940 but pulled out after the beginning of the Sino-Japanese War. Switzerland was next up but couldn't reach agreements, so the venue was moved to Germany. When that country invaded Poland, the entire 1940 Olympic Games were cancelled and the world went to war.

By 1950 Wilson was the captain of the U.S.Ski Team. His ski jumping prowess was such that he was inducted into the U.S. Ski & Snowboard Hall of Fame and Museum in 1982 and the American Ski Jumping Hall of Fame in 2007.

When the Wilson Memorial Hill, a 50-meter ski jump in Coleraine was dedicated in 1978, Wilson himself was the first rider.

The Coleraine dynasty that rode that hill later would be just as impressive.

The Maki boys started ski jumping when very young. Doug Maki, the younger brother, seems reluctant to give up jumping even now, becoming the ski jumping Masters Division National Champion in 2009. He's been coaching approximately fifty juniors annually in the Coleraine jumping program since 1974.

Older brother Jim Maki has also distinguished himself in the world of ski jumping. In three separate years (1988, 1993 & 1997) Jim was U.S. Masters Level II Champion. It was Jim who represented the Maki family and Coleraine in world competition at both the 1976 Olympics hosted by Innsbruck, Austria and the 1980 Olympic Games in Lake Placid, New York.

Jim Maki was inducted into the American Ski Jumping Hall of Fame in 2008, following in the footsteps of hometown legend, Gene Wilson.

All these accolades should be enough for any town, but Coleraine refuses to give up its bragging rights to ski jumping glory.

Jon Denney moved here from Duluth in the late 1990s and has been the senior

Coleraine Ski Slide

coach for ski jumpers at Coleraine. As a member of the U.S. Ski Team between 1978 & 1985, he was part of the team competing in the 1984 Olympics in Sarajevo. He became notable in ski flying, an extreme version of ski jumping and at one time held the U.S. distance record. Denney's brother, Jim, competed at the 1976 and 1980 Olympics with another dynasty's brother Jim—Jim Maki of Coleraine.

Perhaps, in the case of ski jumping, dynasty is built as much on tradition as heredity.

Lind-Greenway Mine

Jim Maki 1975
U.S. Olympic Ski Jumping Team

Ski jumper

TACONITE/HOLMAN

The story of Holman could be titled either "found and lost" or "came and went" as it was an established community for such a short time.

Founded in 1906, Holman was named for the founder of Holman Mine operated by the Oliver Iron Mining Company.

Although it once had enough population to warrant the Holman School, its major financial base came from the licenses to the large number of saloons. When the Indian treaty provisions were put into effect, saloons were barred from operation and revenues keeping Holman alive disappeared. By 1917 the residents of Holman voted to dissolve the village corporation.

What is left of the little village now sits as a residential area of its former neighbor, Taconite.

Taconite also sat in Indian Territory and as such, didn't, and couldn't, rely on saloon licensing for its revenues. Instead, the Holman Cliffs Mine, an extension of U.S. Steel, provided jobs and financial stability. In fact, once the town was incorporated in 1910, all of the first elected officials worked for Oliver Iron Mining Company, including the policemen.

Holman Mine machine shop

Wide view Holman Mine

Once the ore was depleted in the nearby mines, Taconite, too, lost its luster.

Where once there was a vibrant school life at the Taconite School and numerous residents kept in contact with the outside world via the Taconite post office, a small community looks back at the vitality it had at the turn of the century.

Nearby unused mine pits filled with rain water and run-off and joined what is now called the Canisteo Mine complex.

Holman came and went and while Taconite remains, it only lies quietly as a reminder of a past era.

The loss of profitable mining certainly hurt the residents of Taconite. But the town's people had a greater heartache to come in 1981.

Robert "Beefy" Lawson grew up in Taconite. He became an Itasca County deputy sheriff and was serving under Sheriff Russell Johannsen when he had a run-in with a man he had arrested before.

Audie Fox had two children staying at his parents' home. Lawson was supposed to pick up the children and deliver them to their mother. Upon entering the house, Fox threw Lawson to the floor and shot him to death. That shooting resulted in an 18-hour standoff between Fox and more than sixty law enforcement officials.

Authorities finally apprehended Fox without another shot being fired.

Fox was eventually found guilty of first degree murder and received a life sentence. He has been denied parole three times.

But it's Robert "Beefy" Lawson and his zest for life who is remembered in Taconite - and beyond.

Barkla Family on a summer day!

Taconite Firemen and Fire Trucks

BOVEY

Eric Enstrom put the town of Bovey on the world map. He had owned a photo studio in that town since 1907 when he snapped a photograph that made him, and the little town, world famous.

Enstrom saw something impressive in an old, bearded gentleman who stopped by Enstrom Photography Studio one day in 1918, selling his wares.

Enstrom asked the old man to pose for him at a small table. The old gent, Charles Wilden, sat with his hands folded and head bowed before a Bible on which spectacles rested. Beside that Enstrom placed a bowl, a loaf of bread, and a knife. The scene was set.

Enstrom felt he had a thing of rich beauty after he developed the negative. It took the rest of the world a little longer to realize it. Today the picture "Grace" (a photograph, not a painting as some people believe) is now the Minnesota State Photograph.

Unfortunately for Bovey, that fame didn't translate to fortune. And it certainly could

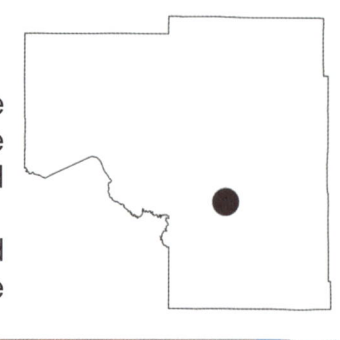

State Auditor Mary Kiffmeyer, MN Senator Bob Lessard, photographer Eric Enstrom's daughter, Rhoda Nyberg, and MN Representative Loren Solberg

Note the pig on Second Avenue

have used it.

Two years after the incorporation of the town named for lumberman, Colonel Charles A. Bovey, a detaching election was held. That resulted in Bovey losing 1840 acres of valuable mineral lands to Coleraine and retaining just 77 acres.

The Bovey area turned its attention to farming. Lands for farming near Riley and Lawrence lakes were opened in 1908 and farm settlements at Trout Lake were expanded.

1908 Bovey baseball team

Scarecrow of "Grace" 2007

In an effort to prove that this was actually an agricultural area, Frank Provinske started Bovey Farmers' Day, held on Labor Day in 1912. Those early affairs consisted of produce displays, lectures, and picnics.

Modern celebrations feature parades, foods, games, and reminiscences of times gone by.

Doug Deal owner of Bovey Press newspaper 1948

Bovey Farmers' Day parade

TALMOON

Three roads converged in a mellow wood (apologies to Robert Frost) and they called the spot Hoover's Corner for D. H. Hoover who built his home and business there.

You never heard of it? How about Talmoon or Hayslip's Corner?

Talmoon is an unincorporated community located on the boundary line between two townships - Lake Jessie and Marcell.

Roughly 50 people drive the nineteen miles north from Deer River to call Talmoon home. Others take that drive to visit the "oldest bar in Minnesota", Hayslip's Corner.

When Hoover sold his small establishment to Leo Hayslip in 1930, the new owner began remodeling the store. In 1933 with the end of prohibition, Hayslip traveled to Fitger's Brewery in Duluth and made a deal for a 26 foot mahogany bar, complete with brass rail, and Hayslip's Corner was born.

In 1939 a post office was to be established and a distinct name was desired for the location. From the information that can be gathered, the name Talmoon was derived from the Swedish language and means something like "a piece of land from which pine trees have been removed". There seems to be a bit of confusion about the translation. Regardless, it's Talmoon now.

Just six miles west of Talmoon is the unincorporated community of Spring Lake sitting in Lake Jessie Township. A post office is there and once a rural school there served area students.

Lake Jessie Township itself was organized in 1901 and by 1903 was being served by the Minneapolis and Rainy River Railroad. The advent of automobiles and maintained roads brought about the discontinuation of rail service in 1930.

The U.S. Postal Service made deliveries to the Jesse Lake Post Office, as it was called, between 1909 and 1954.

Numerous resorts dot the shore of the lakes of Lake Jessie Township where visitors enjoy all the pleasures of the Chippewa National Forest.

Talmoon Post office

Jessie Lake Store

FEELEY TOWNSHIP

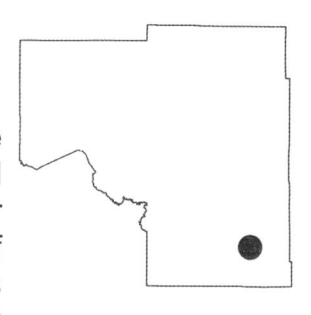

A person who doesn't embrace change might not enjoy the story of Feeley Township. "A rose by any other name would smell as sweet", so says Shakespeare. And that appears to be true for Feeley because it has a history of name changes. As a spur of the Great Northern Railway from 1891 to 1898, the area was simply known as "Siding #8" or "Dickson's Spur". Then in 1899 it became Verna as the Duluth and Winnipeg railroad made its way to the location. That name worked well enough for a Verna School (1901-1903) and the Verna Brick Company. But it didn't last.

Residents decided they needed to continue their growth by becoming an organized township. So, in 1901 Feeley became recognized by the Itasca County Board as a fully organized township. They chose the name "Feeley" to honor the prominent logger and first settler in what is now Warba, Thomas J. Feeley. Once again, the area flourished, even with a third name change. It was Thomas Feeley who first set up a sawmill on the east side of the Swan River in 1898. The area became his namesake. However, as the town itself grew and mail service was put into use, it became apparent that two post offices named Feeley were causing confusion. The town needed a new name and Warba was chosen. Often translated as "White Swan" the Chippewa word "*Warbasibi*" was selected and shortened to Warba.

Great Northern Depot at Warba

Verna Brick Company workers

As with many communities in Itasca County, Warba began as a logging site. Many of its settlers came from Scandinavia. The Swedes, Danes, and Norwegians found the lumber industry and the climate of Itasca County quite similar to what they had known back home.

Incorporated in 1911, Warba saw small business ventures pop up.

Andrew Johnson and A. A. Hall built a small store where the first post office (Verna) would be located. These two, aided by a few others, would establish the Leaf Lumber Company. The Fitger's Brewing Company would erect a three story hotel and the Warba Hardwood Manufacturing Company would build a large sawmill.

School bus circa 1933

Itasca Tie & Cedar Company opened a blacksmith shop in 1908.

In 1914 a bank opened in Warba that would later (1936) move to Grand Rapids acquiring the name Grand Rapids State Bank with Claude Wilcox as president.

Warba has had four different schools with the first classes held in the log house of homesteader Fred Ingersoll. The current school is a charter school called Northern Lights Community School. It uses project-based learning for students in grades six through twelve.

As the timber in the area was depleted, the town of Warba began to lose its shine. Farming replaced the fallen trees, but with no industry supporting the community, it became a sleepy little burg.

Now Warba sits in the township of Feeley. However, they each managed to develop distinct personalities. The folks of Feeley Township are an independent bunch. The Feeley school operated from 1903 to 1916. Feeley cemetery was put into service in 1916. Tichenor and Sand Lake schools served Feeley Township. And Feeley had its own town hall. The Feeley baseball team was organized. The 4th of July celebration in Feeley Township was complete with fireworks.

Warba may be the town but Feeley gave birth to that town. And Feeley Township by any other name would be as sweet.

Warba sawmill

45

ARDENHURST

Just north of Alvwood Township sits the community of Bergville in Ardenhurst Township. It sometimes seems that a community would give itself a name just to have something to call its school or post office. This would appear to be the case of Bergville, where once a school existed and not much else.

The same may be said for the township itself.

Originally, the name Island Lake was selected for the township and settlers sought to establish a post office under this name. The post office department refused that application since there already was a post office in Minnesota by that name.

In 1902, Ardenhurst (meaning "home in the forest") Township was incorporated. But by that time E.C. Cunningham had permission to operate a post office at his place and that's how it became the Cunningham Post Office. He also gave his name to the school.

Other than as an identifier on a plat map in the northwest corner of Itasca County, Ardenhurst seems to have been used only to name the Ardenhurst Township Hall which had once been the Third Bergville School.

And round and round it goes.

Bergville sawmill

Ardenhurst homesteaders working at Blackduck Hotel

Making beautiful music in the Northwoods

BIGFORK

Winding your way northward on Highway 38, you gain a meaningful perspective for the term "Edge of the Wilderness". Perhaps that's why it's almost a shock to suddenly drive out of the woods and into downtown Bigfork.

The town may have been incorporated in 1907 but it became a settlement in 1892 when Damase Neveaux, known as "Uncle Tom", built a log cabin there and laid claim to a tract of regal pines.

After that, the town of Bigfork was created by loggers. The early 20th century saw large timber enterprises develop the area. The Big Fork River, running through the town and nearby pine groves, allowed loggers a means of getting millions of feet of timber to mills in Kenora, Baudette, and other sites.

Bigfork City Hall built by WPA

The Big Fork River provided much more than a handy way for loggers to get product to mills. It was a prolific producer of wild rice. Frank L. Vance recognized this in the early 1890s. He not only built what is considered the first wild rice processing mill in Minnesota; he invented a reaper for harvesting the valuable grain.

Alas for Vance, a ban was soon put on using mechanical means to harvest wild rice. He went out of business when he couldn't profit by picking rice the way the Chippewa had always done it; bend the stalks over and knock the grains into a canoe.

The canoe was not used solely for collecting rice. It allowed for far-reaching travel up and down the Big Fork River and its tributaries. Surely the Native Americans of the Big Fork Valley had used birch bark canoes for centuries. Yet, there was, in this century, a white man who came to appreciate that mode of travel. Bill Hafeman learned

Haying season twice a year!

Tote team to help pioneers move into Bigfork

47

the skills and techniques necessary to build authentic birch bark canoes. Many notable people including Lady Bird Johnson, former First Lady, own his creations. One is also on display at the Itasca County Historical Society in Grand Rapids.

Not far from the town of Bigfork is the area once known as "Busti Township". It was so called because it was once the homesite of Chippewa Chief Busticogan.

The township at 62-25 was reserved for Chief Busticogan as a U.S. government land grant. It is said this was a show of appreciation for the Chief's care of white men stricken during a small pox epidemic.

It is also said that Chief Busticogan buried a large sum of gold on his property.

Those who think it would be fun to go looking for that bounty might do well to remember that woolly mammoth tusks have been discovered in Itasca County. Busti's gold has not.

Bill Hafeman

B-29 Story

In the wee hours of Sunday morning, July 15, 1945, eleven members of a B-29 bomber crew made a hasty jump over the wilds of northern Itasca County. The plane was on a training flight out of Pyotte, Texas, and had just completed an exercise in Duluth and was heading for Wolf Point, Montana. The crew soon detected gas fumes and a decision was made to bail out. The pilot set the plane on autopilot and all men evacuated the plane successfully. They landed near Napoleon, Big Bear and Owen Lakes, and the Link Lake Ranger Station coordinated the search and rescue operation. No definite location of where the plane eventually landed has been determined.

Lind Hotel street scene

Logging was dangerous at times

Early Bigfork School

EFFIE

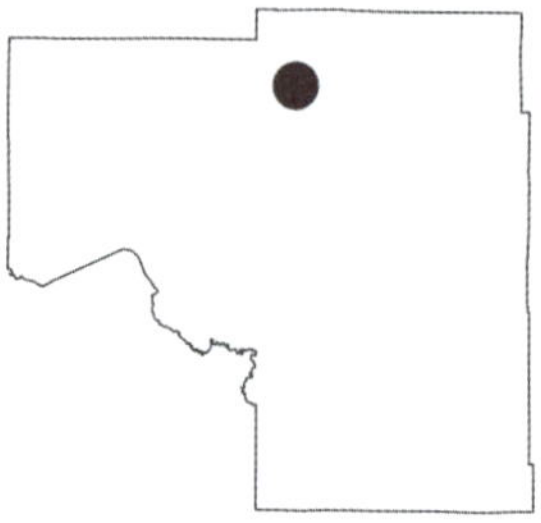

Talk of Northern Itasca County doesn't generally conjure up visions of cowboys and the wild west. But far north in the county there is a community that not only envisions those times, it embraces them.

The Effie community enjoys inviting those who are nostalgic for such things to their summer celebration of the Effie Rodeo and the North Star Stampede. While it doesn't seem to fit in the setting of the north woods, it gives the little community, seven miles north of Bigfork, a unique identity.

That uniqueness would not likely have been found simply by naming the community after the daughter of the first postmistress, Effie Wenaus. Nor by its history as a stop on the Minneapolis & Rainy River Railroad (M&RRR), nor by its proximity to another stop on the M&RRR, Craig (AKA Craigville).

That particular community did not find a unique identity. Craig was a blip on the map and then it was gone, as happened frequently to railroad stops during the early logging days.

It was said that Craig got its name from a well known executive from Grand Rapids.

It was also rumored that the place was an isolated playground for respectable folks.

Taking the long drive from Deer River, Bigfork or Grand Rapids, these prominent people could "whoop it up" in Craig without repercussions from the police (there weren't any) or ramifications from the locals (who were often the providers of the moonshine imbibed!).

Effie Café

Effie Rodeo

You may call Craigville a ghost town today. And if that's the case, only the ghosts up there know the difference between the tales and the truth.

Craig Lumber Mill

49

NORE TOWNSHIP (BRIDGIE/ORTH/HOUPT)

There are small sites in Itasca County that were named mostly for location identification by the railroads serving logging companies. That's one reason you may never have heard of Dexter or Bridgie. They were located in the furthest northwest corner of the county in Nore Township. You haven't heard of that either? No surprise there. The entire population of Nore Township is less than sixty people, just one and a half people per square mile.

Nevertheless, there were enough people to require schools, mail service, and other amenities.

Kittil and Syver Nohre (settlers from Norway) gave their name to the township after it was surveyed in 1894.

Dexter and Bridgie were small communities on the rail line by the early 1900s.

Dexter was later changed to Houpt or Haupt where a school opened in 1911.

Bridgie was named for the first white child born in the area, Bridget Moore. But there was already a Bridgie Township in Koochiching County plus a New Bridgie which became Northome, so this little town turned into Orth. There, a second school was opened which closed in 1942.

The Bridgie Post Office was established in 1895, rescinded and then re-established in 1900 and by 1908 became the Orth Post Office.

Cecilia Hystedt (back right) at Normal School. She would teach at Haupt School

THIRD RIVER/GOOD HOPE/ MOOSE PARK TOWNSHIPS

Townships are generally at least six miles square in area. That does not mean they are equal in stature.

Without a business base or community hub, some townships hold a fascination only for those who live there.

Good Hope, organized in 1908, is one such township. It does have a few lakes including Dunbar, Virgin, Lower Twin, and Sioux which may attract people. Portions of Dixon and Round Lakes also meander into Good Hope Township offering access to resorts and fine fishing.

The community of Dunbar, located there, had enough people to build the Dunbar Lake School in 1918. It was preceded by the Round Lake School in 1910.

Just west of Good Hope Township lies Third River Township with just as little to recommend it. The Decker Lake School was built in 1901, a year before Third River Township was incorporated. That school was replaced by the Rosy School in the community of the same name where a post office was also located.

Both Good Hope and Third River townships had their own cemetery. The Rosy Cemetery sits in Third River and Good Hope Township holds the Dunbar Cemetery.

The third area with just enough to qualify as a township was organized in 1902 and called Moose Park.

Early settlers were mostly from Czechoslovakia and it appears that one of these, Anna Kupcho, was the heart of Moose Park Township. She served as township clerk for twenty-six years, acted as first postmistress when the post office opened in 1919, and delivered more than 120 babies as the local midwife.

Other residents took on important roles by building a school in 1902 and operating the Beighley School from 1919 to 1933. Another school which served the western area beginning in 1933 was called Moose Park.

And, yes, the obligatory Moose Park Township Cemetery reflects the past lives of those who lived in the area.

While these three townships don't jump out as exciting, vibrant metropolises, maybe a better way to view them is as an open frontier in northwest Itasca County just waiting to be explored.

Famous White family house, at one time the Rosy Post Office

NASHWAUK

It is true that trees were more valued in Itasca County than rocks. But that changed in some locations when ore was discovered in the rock and mining became profitable.

The first town in Itasca County to owe its existence to mining was Nashwauk, incorporated in 1903.

By 1917 Nashwauk had twelve mines in operation. The town had a population boom that kept up with the incredible opportunities afforded by all the mining and by 1920 the little town had more than 2000 residents. Likely because of the substantial growth, Nashwauk was the first town on the Western Mesabi Range to have a sanitation system.

Innovation had highlighted life in Nashwauk for years. Water works flowed in 1904 and electric lights shone over the streets in 1906.

Nashwauk is said to mean "land between" and probably was brought to the area by people who emigrated from New Brunswick, Canada where a river of the same name flows.

A small Mennonite community can be found in the Cloverdale district north of Nashwauk. This area is home to numerous farms and is, in fact, referred to as the "Cloverdale farm zone". The Cloverdale School once operated in this district of Nashwauk Township and the Primary School had an enrollment of children from nearly fifty farm families.

In more modern times, the Federal Aviation Administration constructed the Nashwauk Radar site in 1979. Its purpose was to control civilian air traffic in Northern Minnesota for a radius of 280 miles. The fiberglass dome measuring fifty-five feet in diameter sits atop a seventy-five foot tower just north of Nashwauk.

Born from mining endeavors, Nashwauk was the first town in Itasca County where someone kicked a rock - and found it was made of money.

Early settlers

Note Nashwauk's wooden sidewalks

52

KEEWATIN

Awards are not given for what might have been. If they were, the town of Keewatin may well be the champion of Itasca County.

Incorporated in 1906, Keewatin owes its growth to mining. It's only five miles from Hibbing, but is actually located in eastern Itasca County. It sits on rich iron ore deposits of the Mesabi Range. That's what created the incredible wealth of the small town.

Keewatin was one of those lucky places that was located at the right place at the right time.

The early 1900s saw a meteoric rise in mining operations. Technology was making extraction more efficient, ore concentrators improved quality, and capable personnel were available to fill the increasing need for man power. And the Keewatin area was ready.

Mississippi Mine

St. Paul Mine started operations in 1905 and would enjoy the position of sole mining venture in Keewatin until 1908 when the Bray Mine opened.

These mines soon required rail service to meet the demands of their operations. Great Northern Railroad met that requirement by extending service to Keewatin in 1909. Once that happened, more companies could "make tracks" to Keewatin. And so they did. Within a year, the Bennett and Mississippi mines started up.

It should be obvious then, how Keewatin became the richest city in Itasca County by 1911.

Nothing lasts forever. Other cities were seeing economic growth and population booms that would undermine (no pun intended) the status once enjoyed by Keewatin.

However, with the opening of Keewatin's largest mine, the Mesabi Chief in 1927, Keewatin was again a thriving community.

But mining is a notoriously up and down business venture. Sometimes supply and demand plays a role while other times it's international trade or diminished resources that have an effect on a specific industry.

1913 Dray for People's Brewing Company

Keewatin received one more upswing with the construction of National Steel Pellet Taconite processing facility. In 1974 a group of companies joined forces to invest in the plant known locally as Keetac. That facility has seen the ups and downs in mining as well.

It needs to be said that Keewatin had –

4th of July Parade

and still has – more personality than just day-to-day mining concerns.

The Great Northern passenger train known as the "Merry Widow" ran over to Duluth until it ended rail service to Keewatin in 1924. It gave the locals access to the "big city". A boxcar served as the first depot.

The people of the town were civic minded, choosing to pass the first traffic ordinance in 1914. That ordinance limited motor vehicles to a speed of 8 miles per hour in town. The townspeople erected guard houses and fences around the school to keep horses and cows off the grounds. They even had an early interest in ecology, proven by the 1942 Salvage Committee fund raiser recycling paper, tin cans, and rubber.

Even today, Keewatin is a Star City, meaning there are citizens promoting economic growth.

So don't give Keewatin the "potential only" award just yet.

Celebration by the wood expansion bridge over Steven's Pit

ALVWOOD TOWNSHIP

Should you drive 13 miles east of Blackduck or ten miles south of Northome, you might enter a settlement called 13 Mile Corner. Then again...by 1905 that location was called Alvwood with its own post office, even though it was never incorporated as a town.

Alvwood Township was wired for telephones by the fall of 1915. The Alvwood school closed in 1941 and the students were transported to nearby Dunbar school. By 1952 all the area students attended the school in Squaw Lake.

These tiny towns spring up and fade away throughout Itasca County year after year in the early 1900s. In reality, Alvwood lost more than half its population between 2000 and 2010 census. But those stalwart residents prove the tenacity of the early settlers who found Itasca County to be a place to call home.

Inside one room schoolhouse

Early Homesteaders

SAGO TOWNSHIP

If there is such a term as "momentary history", Sago Township and its communities would define it.

Sago Township was home to rail stops on the Hill City Railway Company, to schools, and even to a post office. But they were gone almost as fast as they were established.

John A. Leipold was given permission to operate an official post office at his place and LEIPOLD became a legal post mark in 1908.

The Hill City Railway Company offered tickets to and from Rabey, Seaver and Leipold, none of which remain today.

The Harrington School opened in 1905 but was replaced by the Leipold School in 1922. In 1913 another building was erected to house the Maki School which was part of School District #1, but actually located in Wawina Township.

Families came and went to Sago Township like trains making stops and moving on. And though it was incorporated in 1903, and exists today, Sago Township embodies the words "momentary history".

Leipold School #2 circa 1923

Passenger train at Swan River

Swan River Train Depot

Afternoon ride?

SWAN RIVER

Sometimes in settling an area the railroads were the impetus for making a place into a community. So it was with Swan River.

Set up as a base camp while constructing a line from Duluth to Pokegama Falls, the Duluth and Winnipeg Railroad brought vitality to Swan River area. It sat as a depot at the junction where the Duluth, Mississippi River and Northern Railroad met the Duluth and Winnipeg.

It was a natural spot for a hotel and a great place for Thomas Feeley to put up a saloon and sawmill.

In 1894 Feeley moved his operation to "Feeley's Spur" which would later become Warba when "Verna" and "Feeley" merged in 1911.

In 1895 Swan River residents organized townships into Swan River Township. That plan was ill conceived and the township was dissolved, later to be organized into Sago and Wawina Townships. So it is that Swan River, the community, sits in Sago, the township.

Swan River was not without notoriety. Before the turn of the century (the one where 1800 turned into 1900!), Swan River provided three county commissioners John F. Killoran, Henry Logan, and John Rellis to local government. And such magnificent pines grew in the area that during the Eisenhower administration, the National Christmas Tree came from Swan River.

With the decline in logging and no use as a railroad stop, Swan River is once again just a quiet little place in southeastern Itasca County.

Truck stop circa 1957

Swan River provides National Christmas Tree

Logging operation

GOODLAND TOWNSHIP

Even the smallest community can have a large and interesting history. Goodland is such a place.

The Great Depression of the mid-1930s was taking a toll on the availability of jobs and people living in the cities were hit hard. One man devised a plan to fight the poverty of city life by creating a communal farm colony at Goodland. Eathan Allen (not to be confused with Ethan Allen the patriot) gathered a group of others living in the Twin Cities and, with a government loan, began building the colony. The group built roughly twenty cabins. Barns were erected to house cattle and poultry. Crops included rutabagas, potatoes and hay.

As with most communal living projects, dissension began to dismantle the colony. In the end there were only four families left at the Goodland Colony.

Goodland Township was organized in 1904. The town site of Goodland began as a station of the Great Northern Railway under the name of Gardner.

That name was changed to Goodland when C.H. Phinney's company purchased the site.

The little unincorporated village featured schools, general stores, plus a post office which opened in 1903 that still serves the Goodland residents.

Goodland Post Office

Goodland train depot

KINGHURST TOWNSHIP

Experts who study world population will tell you we're running out of space. Overcrowding is the catalyst for disease, hunger and personal stress. It's apparent they haven't included Kinghurst Township or Grattan or Pomroy Townships in their studies.

In Kinghurst Township just three people share a square mile while in Grattan Township each person gets their own square mile of land according to census population density reports. Of course, that's not the way populations are situated, but it gives you an idea of the space.

In truth, as much as people may say they want solitude, they tend to congregate. Dora Lake is an unincorporated community where 70% of the residents of Kinghurst Township live. There was once a post office there called Popple, which became Dora Lake in 1946 and operated until 1953.

Dora Lake also had an interesting school. The sections were purchased from Sears & Roebuck (an early mail order catalog) and then erected on the east side of Dora Lake. Once the school closed, the building became the Kinghurst Township Hall.

Being so sparsely populated, the area had schools at other locations as well.

Pomroy got its own frame school after their children hiked four or five miles to the Pinetop School for many years.

The northwest portion of Kinghurst was served by the Orchid School while Robinson School served the south half of the township starting in 1915. By 1921 Kinghurst School took over for Orchid.

From Dora Lake it is forty miles to Deer River and twenty miles to Bigfork, Blackduck or Northome. With that much distance to industry, business and employment it's likely there will be a couple of empty square miles within Grattan, Pomroy and Kinghurst Townships far into the future.

Recess at school

Blueberry pickers

Orchid School

GRATTAN/POMROY TOWNSHIPS

It's interesting that mix ups with the postal service played such a large role in determining names in Itasca County.

Grattan Township was officially organized in 1905 and named for Irish statesman Henry Grattan. The post office, however, was called Pine Top. So was the one just across the county line in Koochiching County. Therefore, the Itasca County site became the Grattan Post Office in 1905.

Next door to Grattan Township sits Pomroy Township. So similar are these locations that they are often considered one area with some going so far as to hyphenate the two into "Grattan-Pomroy". But Pomroy is a separate, unincorporated community which, at one time, had its own school.

Homestead

Grattan Township folks also valued education for their children. They attended classes at the first school housed in a small log shack sitting east of the Torkelson farm. By 1913 they had a good size log structure dedicated as the Pinetop School where teacher (Miss Stella Whipple) and students could concentrate on learning. It wasn't until 1920 that the Grattan School was built and served as an institute of education before closing in 1930.

Those who have never been through Grattan Township are missing one of the most unique areas in Itasca County, in all of the Chippewa National Forest, as a matter of fact.

This little blip on the map is known as the "Lost Forty".

Just as the Pine Top Post Office needed to be changed because of mail mix ups, the "Lost Forty" exists because of a government mix up. In 1882, the Government Land Survey placed the land of the "Lost Forty" in part of Coddington Lake. It was this mapping error that caused these 144 acres to be left untouched by loggers. Over the years these trees matured (some white and red pines there are over 350 years old) into four foot in diameter giants. Even the comparatively short-lived aspens in the "Lost Forty" are over sixty years old.

The area is managed and preserved by the Chippewa National Forest. But hurry if you want to see the unique majesty of the "Lost Forty" before age will cause it to be truly lost.

Majestic pines of the Lost Forty

Lost Forty

MARCELL/STOKES TOWNSHIPS

In the heart of Itasca County you will find what might have been the town of Turtle Lake. Understandably, authorities in 1902 would not allow one more post office to be established using that name, so the application came in calling it Marcell in honor of the first conductor on the Minneapolis & Rainy River Railroad (M&RRR), Andrew Marcell. That same premise followed when the residents petitioned for a township named Big Turtle Lake in 1905 and immediately changed the name to Marcell Township.

The township, early on, was found to have significant stands of white pine lining the shores of Turtle Lake. This was not ignored by the Itasca Lumber Company which quickly laid tracks to the lake from Jessie Junction, later called Alder. On Turtle Lake the Itasca Lumber Company Railroad engaged two steamboats (the Cassie & the Jennie B.) to haul log booms across the lake to the loading tracks.

The railroad connected the area to the outside world until the M&RRR ceased running to Talmoon in 1933. It had been thirty-two years since Itasca Lumber Company had incorporated as the Minneapolis & Rainy River Railroad, often called the "Gut and Liver".

The "Gut and Liver" added stops outside of Marcell to aid logging companies and homesteaders. One such stop was called Jaynes after the first township treasurer, Albert Jaynes.

The area maintained its scenic beauty even after the pines were logged. The fact that Marcell Township includes part or all of forty-eight lakes has also helped it become a resorters paradise.

Next door in Stokes Township, the same holds true. Beautiful resorts, cabins, and summer homes can be found on Horseshoe Lake, west shore of Turtle Lake, Hatch Lake and others.

The similarities come naturally since Stokes was once part of Marcell Township. It was in 1918 that the township divided and Stokes Township took on the northern portion. Both townships are accessible by State Highway 38, aptly known as the Edge of the Wilderness Scenic Byway.

Log hoist

Newstrom Store circa 1930

Near Marcell

SUOMI

Perhaps the similarity in climate or the geographical setting between Minnesota and Scandinavia resulted in the influx of those persons to this state. It could be that settling an area, where summers could be short and steamy, and winters deathly frigid, took a special kind of determined heartiness. Whatever the reason, Scandinavians were not only pleased to establish settlements in Northern Minnesota, they thrived here.

There are homestead entries for the Finnish community of Suomi dating back to 1873, but those were mostly transient timber men with little interest in developing a settlement. Most of those lumberjacks packed up as the Minneapolis & Rainy River Railroad (the "Gut and Liver"), which had run since 1898, pulled up in 1904 and re-routed to Jessie Junction (later Alder). It was the Finns who made Suomi, which means "Finland", a real community.

Within two years of their arrival, these folks had established the Suomi Evangelical Lutheran Church where services were held in their native Finnish language.

Three years after the church began, the Suomi Post Office was established with Mrs. Urho Rikala as postmistress, likely because the office was housed in Rikala's store. The post

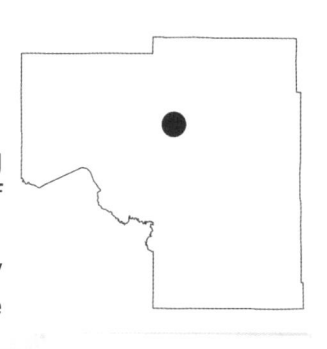

Road improvement necessary

Farm work

Summer haying

Strike up the band

Suomi Hills via cross country skis

office was later closed.

Schools also became necessary. Many were held in homes. Physical school buildings were actually erected near the community to accommodate small numbers of students in localized areas. Grave Lake School, for example, boasted only eleven students during the first term. By 1944 the school was closed and eventually all students were attending Deer River School.

In 1925 Suomi School organized its own district - School District #13. But by 1933 it was dissolved and joined District #1. Those students, too, eventually moved on to Deer River schools.

Suomi, at various times, also was home to Suomi Chapter of Minnesota Finnish-American Historical Society, Purchasing Co-op, and Suomi Workers Club.

It may be of interest to note that of all these establishments only the church remains viable to this day. A testament to the determined people and the faith that brought them to Itasca County from the beginning.

Island on Caribou Lake

BEARVILLE TOWNSHIP

Bearville Township was organized in 1906 and is surrounded by unorganized townships, with the exception of Carpenter Township which sits due north. A gold vein had been found just west of Bearville Township inspiring homesteaders to flock to the site. But by 1894 the vein had run out and settlers turned their attention to logging.

About 1904 the town of Bear River, within Bearville Township, was plotted by Lars Brude. Within a year the Nichols School was erected. There would eventually be the Drybridge School and finally the Bear River School serving area families.

"Bear River Journal" covered the area news for five years beginning in 1906. It was all the vision of one Miles Nelson who homesteaded there in 1901. He was the first mail carrier for the Bear River Post Office in 1905. It was Nelson who petitioned to have Bearville Township organized.

Fun on the 4th of July

Drybridge School

1912 shingle cutting bee in Bearville

TOGO

Tiny communities sprang up across Itasca County. The fact that some are unorganized or never incorporated doesn't change the fact that they are there - or that they play a role in the county's history. A perfect example is Togo. The town's motto is: "Where the pavement ends, and the north begins". Togo sits at the most northeastern corner of Itasca County in Carpenter Township, which was, by the way, formally organized in 1906. The boundary line between Itasca, St. Louis, and Koochiching counties intersects very near Togo.

This remote community once had its own elementary school. It also housed a post office. It was, in fact, the first postmaster, Miles A. Nelson, who named the town after Admiral Togo of the Japanese navy, which sank the Russian fleet during the Russo-Japanese War in 1905. Today Togo has less than 15 people per square mile.

The tiny locale became home to *Thistledew Camp*, a juvenile correctional facility established in 1955 by the Minnesota Department of Corrections. There is also a women's correctional facility there operating as a boot camp for adult

"one horse open sleigh"

1912 threshing outfit

women offenders. The name *Thistledew Camp* was changed to *Minnesota Correctional Facility -Togo* in 2015.

The greatest claim-to-fame for the small community may very well be that it is the rearing and training ground for champion sled dogs and their master, Jamie Nelson. Not only has Nelson braved the Alaskan Iditarod Trail Sled Dog Race four times, but she is the four-time winner of the John Beargrease Sled Dog Marathon in 1988, 1995, 1997 and 1998. The "Beargrease" is the longest sled dog race in the lower 48 states at nearly 400 miles in length and runs along the North Shore of Minnesota.

Nelson and business partner, Ann Stead (who also runs a kennel with her husband Al) run Mushing Bootcamps and Pull Training Clinics in Oregon, Colorado, Michigan, New York state and, yes, Togo, Minnesota.

First self binder

Postcard from Nass

WIRT

Sometimes it's hard to imagine a small, virtually disappearing town could have once been a thriving, bustling settlement. Just one example of such a community is the town of Wirt on the Bigfork River.

The community now sits at the site of a former logging town called Stanley. It was named for William Wirt by Elias Walley, the acknowledged first white settler in town. Wirt was appointed by President Thomas Jefferson as the prosecuting attorney in the trial of Aaron Burr in 1807 who was charged with treason. Wirt later served as United States Attorney General for twelve years.

It is obvious that early settlers did not discover the area. By definition "discover" means "to be the first to find out about or see." That right belongs to the Mounds Indians of the Sioux. Some of those mounds reveal a Sioux presence in the area as early as 600 A.D. But by 1748 the Chippewa had driven the Sioux further west and claimed the land. The current location of Wirt is not on the Chippewa Reservation, however. And by 1905 Wirt boasted an immigrant population of twenty-one residents.

That was also the year that the Minneapolis & Rainy

Wirt Post Office

Logging Break - well cared for tools

River Railroad (M&RRR) extended their line to Wirt to deliver mail and supplies, transport people, and most importantly, to accommodate timber companies. With the extension of railroad service, Wirt actually became two towns. Stanley housed the railroad depot and was a busy logging town, but the store to the west had a Wirt address. By the time the M&RRR was removed in 1931, Wirt was all that existed.

Although 1922 saw passable roads extending from Wirt to Sand Lake and west to Bigfork, the end of the railroad might have been the end of the small community.

Then, in 1934, President Franklin Roosevelt initiated a public works program of Civilian Conservation Corps (CCC) camps to combat the effects of the Great Depression. Just two miles outside Wirt, a CCC Camp, which included a large barracks, offices, a kitchen, and hospital, was established. The influx of workers, paid roughly $30 monthly, infused new vitality to Wirt's economy. This upswing would be short-lived as the CCC camp workers were called to service at the start of World War II and the CCC camps became obsolete.

So many small locales sprang up for reasons specific to their features. The woodlands around Wirt were enough to attract numerous lumbermen. The river, then the railroad, made it possible for the community to thrive and prosper from its natural resources. And, as with innumerable communities grown by specifics, Wirt is truly becoming a part of the history of Itasca County.

1903 Engine No. 1

CCC Camp entrance

CCC Camp Bunkhouse

BALSAM/LAWRENCE TOWNSHIPS

Grandma Brandon was the county's oldest living resident when she died at age 105 in 1958. The David Brandons had moved to Balsam Township in 1906.

It was the Charles V. Smith family who first came in 1903. Smith built a three-story log house in 1907 which became a famous stopping place. On one single night the Smiths slept eighty-four men. It continued to be a social hub of Balsam Township until it burned down in 1957.

The creation of the township is a story in itself. The area didn't have a large enough tax base to build a road to Bovey, the nearest town. So the residents combined the area of four townships including East & West Balsam, Wabana, and Lawrence Lake into Balsam Township. Once organized in 1907 it was now able to be bonded for $20,000 to construct the twenty-mile road. Lawrence would detach from Balsam Township in 1920 and Wabana would follow suit in 1921.

Balsam Township was prolific in its school building. In 1911 it was the Sunrise School, followed by the Shumaker School which closed in 1953. The 1920s gave rise to the Hansen Lake, Cloverdale, the first and second Smith School, and Big Balsam School which closed in 1943. In 1924 the Kinnunen School became the Lower Balsam and closed by 1953 when Balsam Elementary School was built.

The expansive Joyce Estate sat on Trout Lake in Balsam Township. Once a

1907 famous stopping place---Smith House

Balsam School 1912

First car in the area (Buick)

summer get away for the family and friends of Chicago lumber baron, David Joyce, the Joyce Estate boasted a landing strip, a greenhouse, tennis courts, and a golf course for the amusement of visitors.

Interesting characters are part of the Balsam Township tale. There's Tony DeWire who ran the steamboat on Lake Wabana of which it is said, "It was used to haul logs and to haul supplies. It came and went, always leaked and never sank - but once."

You had "Old Put" the master boat builder who was really George N. Putnam and really good at telling tall tales.

Telling tales also seems to be the talent of "Bunga" (there is a discrepancy in how that's spelled) Buck", a half Negro, half Chippewa, who claimed to be the first "white man" in the area.

Once a land covered with balsam fir, the township drew its name from the extremely beautiful trees and was home to the small, unincorporated community of Martin.

First frame house in Balsam Township

Joyce Estate

Homestead at Snaptail Lake

ARBO TOWNSHIP

It's been said, "you can't be in two places at the same time". However, there was a hiccup in time when that wasn't quite true.

In 1905 both George and James Affleck, along with John Arbo, were a few of the small number of residents in the area. In June of 1907 "Prairie Lake" township was officially organized, but within a week the township was being called Arbo township, named for John Arbo.

However, as late as 1917 there was an Affleck post office and even the local newspaper referred to the area as "Affleck". Soon after the newspaper was referring to the township and community by its proper name of Arbo and the mix up seems to have ended.

Arbo Township grew along with the timber industry. In fact, most of the early land owners were logging companies. Perhaps the most expansive of these was Price Brothers who, at times, would have more than 3000 men on their payrolls.

This company knew how to make use of the Prairie River and built dams, including the one at the lower end of Prairie Lake.

The last of the timber drives on the Prairie River occurred in 1928. For some townships that would have been the beginning of a disappearing act.

Prairie River Dam

This was not the case for Arbo Township.

The residents of Arbo saw many reasons and methods for keeping their area lively and vibrant.

In the early 1920s work began on a road from Grand Rapids to Marcell and by the 1930s what had been known in the township as Prairie River Road was called Highway 38 giving great access to the township.

Swinging at Gunn Park

Blandin Paper Company developed Gunn Park on Prairie Lake opening a pleasant recreation area for public use. About the year 2000 the park was taken over by Itasca Little League while the maintenance of the pavilion rests with the county.

Another unique recreational pastime came courtesy of the Arbo Hockey Team in the 1930s. The team played on a rink on Arbo Lake and had an ingenious homemade Zamboni to keep the ice in playing condition. The workers would fill the barrel with water and the pipe below had holes in it. They attached a sack to the pipe, which would help spread the water.

Homemade Zamboni for Arbo Hockey Team

Further means for recreation in Arbo Township came when a land use plan was written allowing the Prairie River gorge and the tailing ponds to be retained for biking and hiking trails.

Bridges over the Prairie River allowed roads to criss-cross Arbo Township giving access to all the sights (and sites) that give the area its charm.

Timber drive on Prairie River

GREENWAY TOWNSHIP

When looking at history there are occasionally people you seem to run into all over the place.

John C. Greenway was instrumental in designing the town of Coleraine. He also planned and administered the opening of the Canisteo District for Oliver Mining Company on the Western Mesaba Range.

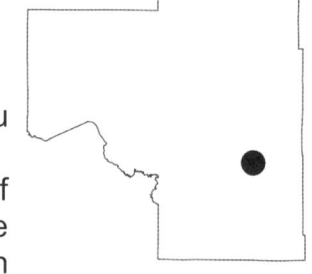

Greenway already had a striking reputation by the time the township was named for him in 1909.

He had been a baseball and football star when he was president of his class at Yale. And he distinguished himself so well as one of Teddy Roosevelt's Rough Riders, he was commissioned a first lieutenant by Roosevelt.

The mines in the area required workers and workers needed houses and a place to live. Some small communities, no more than a row of houses, quickly grew and almost immediately disappeared; places with names like Cooley, Release, Holman, Cort, Jurgenson, and Noyes.

While the mines produced ore and the Great Northern Railroad charged for use of its rails that ran through, Greenway Township found wealth like few other places in Itasca County.

Hill Annex Mine

1910 Sinking Test Pit

John C. Greenway

MARBLE

Perhaps the old saying should go, "you can't see the mining for the trees". That appears to be true, especially for locations on the western end of the Mesabi Range, and Marble was no exception.

From 1890 until 1910 the Bovey-DeLaittre Lumber Company managed to operate in Marble. But by 1901 an ore sample from the Arcturus Mine was sent for testing, found favorable and mining took off.

Once again it was the Superintendent of the Canisteo District, John C. Greenway, who oversaw the surveying of the Village of Marble into streets and lots.

Hill Mine steam shovel 1908

The construction of the Duluth, Missabe and Northern Railroad through Marble opened the Walker, Canisteo, Holman, and Hill mines to rail shipment.

Named for R.N. Marble, a U.S. Steel official, the town saw such growth that the

Tent city

74

population overflowed into a tent city about a half mile north. It may have been the white color of the tents that gave the location its name - White City.

Of note, the Hill mine was located within the village limits of Marble. That is significant because at one point, the Hill mine was the richest in the world and that made Marble the "ten million dollar village"!!

Barber shop

"Alice in Wonderland" at Fairyland

Hill Mine 1908

Taken by Durant Barclay in Marble 1906

CALUMET

The languages of Native Americans probably had the most impact on the names settlers gave to areas than any other source.

Calumet was the name given by the French to the reed-stemmed "peace pipes" of the Native people. When the town was incorporated in 1909 that name was chosen.

Once logging had been replaced by mining, accommodations were needed for workers, so Calumet was created.

The Duluth, Missabe and Northern Railway built a line through the area in 1906 hauling ore to world ports.

For the locals, it was the Great Northern Depot in Calumet that was exciting. There, in the summer, they could hop on the "Blueberry Special" which ran from Coleraine to Duluth. They could take the train to a favorite blueberry patch, fill their pails with berries and return home that evening.

Residents of Calumet didn't merely watch the world go by.

In 1942, during World War II, Vladimir Shipka organized the "Johnny Doughboy Club". Shipka, who would later become a State Senator, decided to do something to meet the needs of local servicemen serving abroad.

Trolley at Hill Annex Mine

Pouring first sidewalks in Calumet

Funds were raised annually during Johnny Doughboy Days celebrations to send gifts to servicemen. A "Letters From Home" committee was formed to keep the boys in touch with the home front.

The Johnny Doughboy Club of Calumet is the only club known by that name in the world.

Hill Annex Mine office

Johnny Doughboy Days parade

BLACKBERRY

Blackberry Township was organized in 1909, but the community of Blackberry began much earlier.

As with so many locales, it was the railroad that determined population distribution. When the Great Northern railroad came through the area in 1890, it's likely that the section foreman, Peter Larson, noticing the plethora of blackberries, named the site. However, it was Ora M. Harry who built a log store in 1899, and became the first postmaster and started creating a viable community.

The people of Blackberry trusted that the railroad would establish a depot at their location. But Great Northern provided nothing more than a boxcar for a depot and never assigned a local agent, despite the fact that one season nearly sixty carloads of potatoes were loaded at the site.

There was the Blackberry Store and another shop that would evolve into Happy Hollow, to serve the needs of residents.

Murphy Mercantile

Bridge at Blackberry

Murphy Mercantile

HARRIS TOWNSHIP

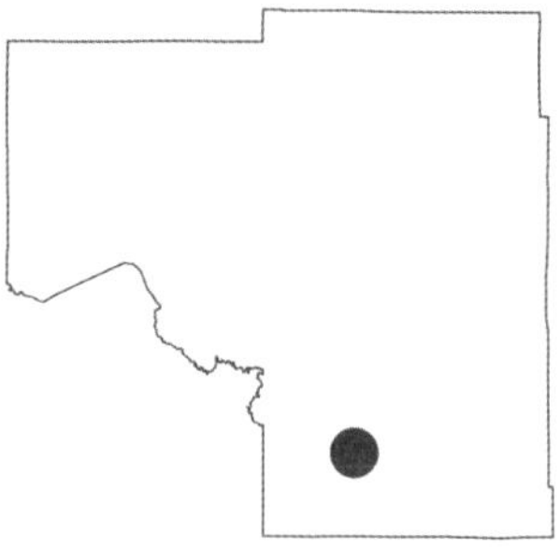

Cedars and maple trees, tall pines touch blue skies. An arm of Pokegama Lake holds on to a sandy shore. Seclusion and solitude abound.

That wasn't a 21st century real estate brochure. It's what Duncan Harris found when he set up a farm in the 1880s. The township was named for this first farmer of the area even though the township wouldn't be incorporated until 1909.

When Harris arrived, the Chippewa were still living near Pokegama Lake. The truth is that the Chippewa did not release their reservation around Pokegama Falls until 1863 and many of them remained in the area. To them, Harris was more an interloper than a welcome neighbor. To be fair, when someone shows up and begins tapping the maples you relied on for syrup, starts clearing forests you found wild game in, and takes fish from the water you revered, your inclination is not to make friends. Harris managed to coexist and made a truce of sorts, to the extent that his wife occasionally fed the Indians as they traversed the land near the Harris homestead. By the time Harris died in 1922, when a tree he had cut fell on him, the area was well settled.

The "Onawa" on Pokegama Lake

One community became known as Wendigo, meaning "evil spirits" in the Chippewa language. The settlers were apparently not superstitious and soon they found they had enough children to warrant school facilities. To begin with, eight children attended the Carlson School, so named because it sat near "Grandpa" Carlson's residence. By 1916 it was moved to the D.A. Grussendorf farm.

With the growing number of students in need of an education in 1917, School District #1 decided to build a school at the southeast end of Pokegama Lake. The

Personette Farm circa 1920s

Mrs. Duncan Harris

Wendigo School of 1917 housed a library and two classrooms on the second floor with the furnace room, lunch room, and manual training room on the ground floor.

Around 1922 schools were being consolidated and the students from Liebrick School on the River Road, which closed that year, were now attending Wendigo School.

As late as the 1980s children filled the school yard of the Wendigo School for recess. And the only "evil spirits" to be found were the school boys who pulled girls' pigtails.

Highway 169 crosses Pokegama Lake

"Your life vest is slipping!"

Wendigo School

WAWINA TOWNSHIP

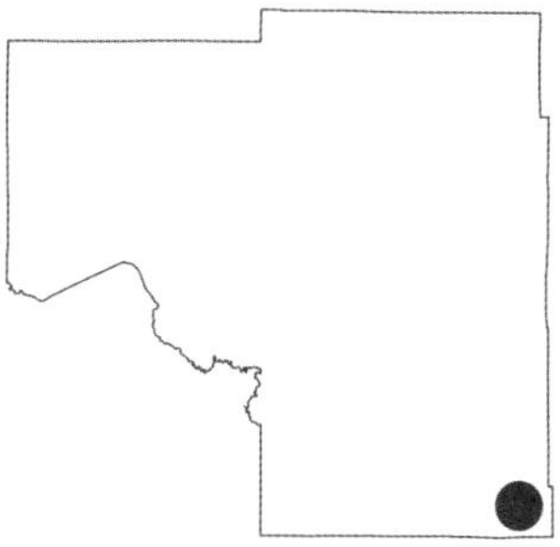

Like so many communities, Wawina began with logs and schools. When Eric Hakala and John Lyly came to the area from Finland, they found it covered in forest. Logging became the main occupation by 1900.

Almost immediately a school was built where Miss Fletcher would teach in 1901. That was followed by the Westfork School in 1908. Finally, the Wawina School was erected near town and operated between 1916 and 1946.

More families moved into the most southeastern township of Itasca County during 1933 when Highway #2 was being built. Those families wanted a little culture in their lives, so in 1939 Wawina residents organized their own orchestra.

From a whistle stop on the Duluth and Winnipeg Railroad known as Siding #6 to a refined little community, Wawina Township holds a place in county history.

Oaks farm 1905

Carlson's Store circa 1920

Farming in Wawina

Merikanto Store circa 1930s

SPANG TOWNSHIP

When you think of Spang Township you think farming community. However, when it was incorporated in 1911, Spang was more of a logging area. During one spring in the early 1910s more than 25 million feet of logs were sluiced in Dinnerpail Lake alone.

Large lumber companies like Weyerhauser and Bovey-DeLaittre worked the area during the great logging days of 1880 to 1905. Around 1905 there were numerous roads in Spang Township. A tote-road ran through from Hill City to Grand Rapids. Another went around the west end of Pokegama Lake to Cohasset and on to Grand Rapids. Another road went east through Wendigo to the River Road and then north to Grand Rapids. But whichever course you chose, it was a thirty-eight mile trek from Spang to Grand Rapids until the ferry was put in at Pokegama Lake.

The ferry was a slow process. The oxen had to be unhooked from the load and made to swim across. And, until a gas engine was installed to power the ferry, it was hauled hand over hand by Loren "Old Pete" Hane. So ineffective was the ferry that it closed down by 1921.

By 1916 settlers were claiming the cleared land for farms.

Charles A. Olson was the first permanent settler in Spang Township when he came from Iowa in 1903. As a carpenter he was kept busy building homes for newcomers as well as hotels and school buildings.

Others came to Spang Township and began farming. Men like Anton Benes (1904), Ernest Foix (1906), Olaf Jellum (1910), Ed Peterson (1911), and William Kutcher (1915) began farms and families in Spang; some of those families continue in the area 100 years later.

Peterson's son, Sampson (Samp), for example, was the first graduate from Spang and was the Spang bus driver for thirty-two years.

As a bus driver Peterson was kind but firm. It was said that "Some kids have to be paid to be good. The kids on Samp's bus were *good for nothing*"!

That humor and work ethic exemplifies the nature of the people of Spang Township.

Many city folks think of those early farmers as backward, less educated, or unsophisticated. If you're one of those, you might do well to remember that during the Women's Suffrage Movement in 1917, it was the Maple Lake Farmers Club (later the Spang Farm Bureau) that amended its by-laws to permit "the woman or man at the head of the household to vote and hold office." Rather forward thinking for a bunch of "unsophisticated" farmers, wouldn't you say?

1953 Spang Sunshine Club

1962 Itasca County Cake Bake-off winners

COOLEY

..."Now, therefore, you are hereby notified that the said City of Cooley was dissolved on March 21, 1974 and that the last duly constituted governing body of the City of Cooley, formerly the Village of Cooley, shall have custody of any funds of said City from this dissolution until January 1, 1975"...

This public notice was dated September 15, 1974 and signed by W. W. Waite, Clerk of the City of Cooley, formerly Village of Cooley.

But, why?

The shortest answer is that the mines became unproductive. There was no longer a need for the towns that once made jobs in mining a great way of life.

Today if you travel between Pengilly and Nashwauk you will find no sign that Cooley ever existed there. It did, though, and its story is a little complicated so you need to pay attention.

The Butler Brothers entered the area to begin mining at the LaRue Pit. With the building of a line through the Cooley area in 1908, the Great Northern Railroad opened the area for ore shipments.

Building a fort out of community garages

Five short years later they held leases at the Quinn, Harrison, and North Harrison Mines, followed by the Patrick and Kevin Mines. Boarding houses were established near the worksites called "Harrison Location" or "First Cooley". One of the Butler Brothers sons, Cooley Butler, lent his name to this little community. Houses soon sprang up and the Butler Brothers built a clubhouse as a

Butler Brothers Harrison Mine looking south towards Cooley

social center for the men. There was even a water tower and a general store at First Cooley.

Local government came to the area in 1917 with the organization of Lone Pine Township where Cooley sat. That seemed to work just fine until 1921 when it was suggested that Cooley become an incorporated village in its own right. The reason as to the need for this more intimate form of local government can't be found. But it's interesting that the proposed town would be composed of areas in Lone Pine, Greenway, and Nashwauk Townships which just happened to contain most of the lands that concerned Butler Brothers operations.

Regardless of whether it gave Butler Brothers more influence in taxing decisions or would help enhance living conditions for mine workers, Cooley was there…and growing. About a mile west of First Cooley, Butler Brothers decided to build new shop facilities and called the "New Location", "Second Cooley". There were no schools in Cooley and the children were bussed to Nashwauk. Cooley did, however, house the Lone Pine Town Hall for a time. At times it boasted a volunteer fire department, post office, and an Experimental Plant operated by the Mines Experiment Station of the University of Minnesota.

The Butler Brothers headquarters were in Cooley until the operations were taken over in 1948 by Hanna Mining.

Then in 1969 the Harrison Washing Plant was dismantled. As that ore processing method became obsolete, so did the village of Cooley, which, itself, was dismantled in 1974.

2nd Cooley Washing Plant

PENGILLY

After the pines have been removed from the land what can be left?

At the northern end of Swan Lake you would have the unincorporated community of Pengilly.

Until 1907 Pengilly thrived by way of the logging industry. After that time the mines provided jobs and financial stability to families in Pengilly.

While some folks chose to become miners, Ralph Hall offered an alternative by building the Brick Plant in 1907. His venture was successful enough to warrant the addition of the Tile Plant. While both plants existed for just about a decade, they had given Pengilly a little breathing room which in turn allowed for the establishment of a post office.

It is said that a gentleman named Dr. Pengilly helped establish the post office so it was called Pengilly in his honor.

On the other hand, in 1903 there were labor disputes arising among miners. Labor union activists were beginning to make noise. It was one John Pengilly, a captain of the Oliver Mining Company, who notified Oliver president Thomas F. Cole that he had squelched that movement in this area. And it may have been his name that was given to the community.

Sitting so close to numerous boundaries, Pengilly is "shared" by three townships—Greenway, Lone Pine, and Goodland.

The beautiful Mesabi Trail passes by as it links Grand Rapids to Ely. And Swan Lake now offers waterfront residences as well as cabins and summer homes.

So whether you believe it was named for a post office developer or a mining official, know that after the pines, you still have Pengilly.

Logging near Swan Lake

Mike Peluso displays Stanley Cup

Lone Pine Town Hall

MORSE TOWNSHIP

Once separated from Oteneagen, Morse Township found some prosperity as the Great Lakes and Lakehead pipelines came through the area. Businesses on the edge of Deer River sat in Morse Township giving additional revenue.

Other growth spurts continued to happen for folks in Morse Township. The "Potato King", Marvin Schwochert, who operated the Potato Farm & Warehouse, received a contract to provide potatoes for government Civilian Conservation Corps Camps in the 1930s, enhancing opportunities.

As late as 1995 Morse Township formed the Western Itasca Joint Powers with other entities including the cities of Deer River and Zemple and Deer River Township. The priority of this coalition was to encourage new businesses. They were successful enough to entice such businesses as Great Lakes Gas Company, Rajala Timber Company, Gibbs Wild Rice Plant and others.

A township hall, a single church and a small cemetery round out the unassuming township named for Nelson E. Morse.

Rajala Lumber Yard

Wild Rice cured and ready for processing

Packaging for shipment

Gibbs Wild Rice Co. processing rice

OTENEAGEN TOWNSHIP

In a county featuring more than 1000 lakes which sits within a state nicknamed "Land of 10,000 Lakes", it's interesting that Oteneagen Township has none! And more than half of the township is actually federal and state forest.

Back in 1910 when it was organized, it consisted of two townships, Morse and Oteneagen. By 1919 a division was requested. The portion that retained the name Oteneagen Township was in township 146 north and range 25 west. The remainder became Morse Township.

There is also a division in how Oteneagen got its name. One story says William Hulbert, a farmer there, named it for the Ojibwe word meaning "fishing place". Another version says it was named for Chief Oteneagen of the White Oak Band of Mississippi Chippewa who is buried at White Oak Point.

Regardless of how it was named, the township managed to build three schools: Kennedy in 1919, plus the Garden School and West Oteneagen. It also erected the Finn Hall and the Labor Sports Hall where numerous social events were held over the years.

"Gut & Liver" - Minneapolis & Rainy River Railway

Oteneagen Township did have the Jacob Jacobson Cemetery where five burials were recorded but, over the years, only one headstone has ever been found and it read "Jacob Jacobson 1883-1918".

Neighbors come to visit in 1900

86

BOWSTRING TOWNSHIP

Fifteen miles north of Deer River on Highway 6 is Bowstring Township and the unincorporated community of Bowstring. In fact, everything around there is called Bowstring. From the river running into the lake, even the local shop is called Bowstring Store. This is where the locals pick up mail sent to zip code 56631.

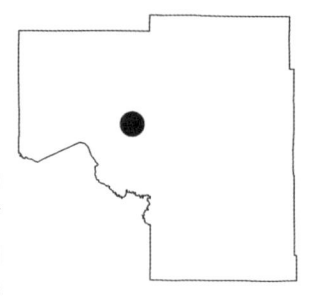

It was in 1902 that W.J. Gibbs built a store which became designated as the first Bowstring Post Office as he contracted with the postal service to run it.

Gibbs moved to the nearby community of Inger in 1910. The town was named for the grandmother of Mrs. Gibbs. Here he built the Riverside Hotel which he lost due to a poor business deal. He then purchased land halfway between Sand Lake and Bowstring Lake where he erected the Inger Store. The establishment served visitors and locals alike for eighty-five years until it closed in 1996.

Today the unincorporated community of Inger rests quietly along the Bowstring River within the Leech Lake Indian Reservation. The quiet is only interrupted by the occasional airplane landing at the Bowstring Airport.

Resort life

Farm circa 1920s

Crossing into Inger

MAX

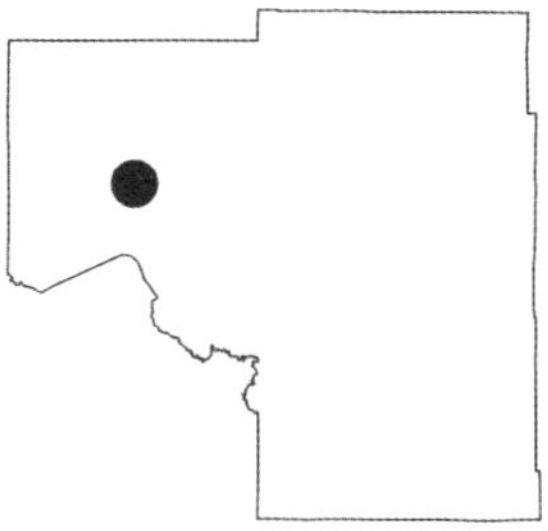

You have been able to send a letter to someone in Max, Minnesota since 1906. Max was also vibrant enough to have a local school from 1919 to 1952. Like so many towns in Itasca County, the first needs to be met were religious and educational with the establishment of churches and schools. Most settlers were equipped to withstand the weather and homesteading necessities, but also believed strongly that the roles of faith and knowledge were crucial to establishing a community.

Max Store circa 1918

Max School 1919-1952

1905 transportation

Round Lake School wood heater

SQUAW LAKE

One could wonder why the community of Squaw Lake is of any interest. Other than the beautiful surroundings of the Leech Lake Reservation or a population where more than 52% of the residents are Native American, what is there that would arouse our curiosity?

For one thing, the Squaw Lake area appears to have been a magnet for schools.

At least seven schools operated in the Squaw Lake area with even more nearby.

There was evidently a school on the east side of Squaw Lake followed by Round Lake School in 1910, Maple Grove School in 1911, the Kananen School from 1913 to 1930, Lepisto School in 1919 and the Squaw Lake School. On the north end of Squaw Lake sat the Teesaker School.

Consolidation by the district in 1951 closed down the nearby schools at Dora Lake, Dunbar, Round Lake, Max and Moose Creek.

It boggles the mind. It's almost as though there was an individual school for each student in the area, especially when you realize the 2010 census put the population number of Squaw Lake at just 107 people!

With the advent of political correctness in the 1990s, controversy intruded on Squaw Lake.

Local students were starting a campaign to end the use of the word "squaw" as they found it offensive.

According to a 1994 article in the St. Paul Pioneer Press titled "Students Seek to Expunge Place Name Squaw," two high school students made an effort to change the names of a reservation, a community and half a dozen lakes containing the word.

Their contention was that "squaw" meant "female sexual parts". However, according to the author of Oxford Etymologist, Anatoly Liberman (as supported by the New World Dictionary of the American Language) the word is derived from the Algonquian and simply means "woman".

The name of the lake was changed to Nature Lake but the town remains Squaw Lake.

Now is there any question as to why Squaw Lake is a place of interest?

"Ring that dinner bell"

Enjoying the afternoon

Community Center 2007

WABANA TOWNSHIP

Wabana Township is a thing of beauty in the heart of Itasca County. Nearly 20% of the township is covered by water. The lakes are dotted with islands.

In 1878 McAlpine and Kirkpatrick came to the area cutting a trail and were followed in 1880 by loggers McAllister and Hasty. It was Itasca Lumber Company that did the majority of logging here between 1889 and 1903. But it was T. H. Simmons, in 1903, who developed Arrowhead Point for summer cabins.

When Dave Cochran moved onto the south shore of Lake Wabana in 1894 he established himself as the first settler and resort man in the chain of lakes.

Cochran had real vision for the waters of Wabana. In 1900 he built a 26 foot steam boat to carry fishing parties over Trout Lake. In 1901, he constructed what was called the Wabana Hotel which operated until 1928 when a fire destroyed the building. He also secured a post office for Wabana.

Others found the islands perfect for summer get aways. Balgillow Island in Wabana Lake was first owned by J. P. Thomson, but by 1929 became the property of "The American Girl". This out-of-the-way girls' camp was conducted by one Miss Mildred Sabo and offered young ladies a northwoods adventure.

Summer fun at American Girl Camp

"Wabana Chief" on Wabana Lake

Sea plane at Wabana Lake

LIBERTY TOWNSHIP

Maps relate history like few other documents. They define current affairs while revealing the past. Maps of Itasca County had to be updated as late as 2015 to maintain accuracy.

Liberty Township sat east of Wirt Township and, in fact, detached from that township in 1922 to establish its own identity by becoming a legally organized township.

The Itasca County 2014 Plat Book shows Liberty Township taking up two 36 square mile plats. By October 2015, that was no longer true, as the township had been dissolved.

There are two ways Minnesota state statutes allow for dissolution of an organized township: do nothing for ten years (including no election of a town board), or a petition can be drawn up to put the question on a ballot. The second option was chosen by residents of Liberty Township. Those residents elected to dissolve the township during the 2014 election.

At that time the formerly organized township had about $50,000 in their coffers, which they decided to allocate for the maintenance of four roads running within the former township's borders. There are very few land owners, with the state and federal governments owning the majority of lands.

Whether the tax base, or the population, decreases in a community, or when disinterest in maintaining local grassroots government occurs, even in this day and age, organized townships can dissolve. And do.

Hunting in the early days.

WILDWOOD/SPLITHAND TOWNSHIPS

Wildwood Township, with nearly 200 residents, wasn't formally organized until 1989. That's not a typo. It was 1989.

Another township late to the party is Splithand which was organized in 1985.

Early on, the tight knit farming community made good use of the fishing lakes in the area. George Moody developed his place into the first resort in 1904.

Others concentrated on potato farming or raising dairy cattle. These folks formed a chapter of Producers Market Association which was the predecessor of the Farm Bureau.

Splithand Township has had five different schools over the years, with the first named school being Cowhorn School in 1902. None of these exist anymore.

Blandin Paper Company owns one half of the land in Wildwood Township. Roughly one quarter of Splithand Township is also owned by Blandin Paper Company while another quarter of Splithand is Itasca County tax forfeited land. All these lands offer access to the public for recreation and hunting.

Cowhorn School at Splithand

Wildwood Township Hall

Old Cowhorn School

Farming in Splithand circa 1975

92

BALL CLUB

There are unique locations within the county that have a great significance beyond what is obvious.

The unincorporated community of Ball Club is certainly one of those.

Its largely Native American population of the Leech Lake Band of Ojibwe find themselves living within the Leech Lake Indian Reservation and the Chippewa National Forest.

The culture and traditions of the indigenous people remain intact with authentic celebrations, ceremonies, and festivals at the powwow grounds.

Ball Club lies on the border of Itasca and Cass counties.

Sitting at the south end of Ball Club Lake, the community was once a railway village with a designated post office.

Today one of its important roles is as a census-designated place (CDP). Simply explained, a CDP is a place of concentrated population identified by the United States Census Bureau for statistical purposes.

Every ten years a census is taken in this area as a counterpart of incorporated towns or cities. These statistics give important information about diversity, households and economics that might otherwise be missed.

Ball Club Lake has a shape resembling the bat used in an Indian game the French called La Crosse, hence its name and that of the community.

Providing its residents with a clinic, community center, as well as social services and education, Ball Club continues to be a unique location of significance in Itasca County.

Canoe at Ball Club

Ball Club Pow Wow

Indian Reservation ceremony

LEECH LAKE INDIAN RESERVATION

Linguistics matter in a discussion of the Indian people of Itasca County. Understanding the words makes a difference; especially when the history is researched and/or told by a white man.

Only two Indian Reservations are located, in part, in Itasca County. One of them holds great significance within the Minnesota Chippewa Tribe.

The Indian Reorganization Act of 1934 merged Leech Lake, Cass Lake, & Lake Winnibigoshish reservations of the Pillager Band along with the Chippewa Indian Reservation of Lake Superior Band and White Oak Point Reservation of the Mississippi Band of Chippewa to form the present "Greater Leech Lake Indian Reservation". The reservation, which is the largest in total area in Minnesota, enters portions of Itasca, Cass, Beltrami, and Hubbard counties. It also registers as the largest Indian Reservation in the state by total number of residents.

While Itasca County houses most of the communities on Leech Lake Reservation, the largest community of Cass Lake is located in Cass County and is the site of Leech Lake Tribal Government.

The fact that nearly all of the reservation land is situated in the Chippewa National Forest enhances the reverence with which the Indigenous People hold the "Earth Mother". Their respect for the land and water that is their Native heritage continues to be taught to each new generation. And, in fact, the Chippewa language is part of the curriculum in many reservation schools and colleges.

Watching the ceremony

Ceremonial Dancing

BOIS FORTE

Most Itasca County residents are aware of the existence and location of the Leech Lake Indian Reservation which begins near Deer River.

However, not all realize that the Bois Forte Reservation also locates in extreme northern Itasca County.

If a land is not inhabited by any Band members, is it still part of a reservation? Yes, because the Deer Creek section of Bois Forte was established by treaty in 1866. It belongs to the Bois Forte Band of Ojibwe also known as Chippewa.

The reservation is divided into three sectors. While no Band members reside in the Itasca County Deer Creek section, the section around Nett Lake in St. Louis County is home to the majority of Bois Forte Band members. It is said to be the largest producer of wild rice in the nation.

The Vermillion sector, near Tower in St. Louis County, is home to Fortune Bay Resort and Casino which opened in 1986. It employs more than 500 people and provides over $30 million to the northern Minnesota economy.

Bois Forte, meaning "strong wood", is governed by the Bois Forte Reservation Tribal Council.

Wild Rice Season

IJC/ICC/AG SCHOOL

It would have been impossible for one location in the State of Minnesota to offer all the features used in the state's vast agricultural endeavors. For that reason, the Minnesota Agricultural Experiment Station, established in 1885, requested and was granted, funds via a Minnesota legislative bill to operate two branch experiment stations. One was begun in Crookston in 1895 and named the Northwest Experiment Station and the second started in Grand Rapids in 1896 and was known as the Northeast Sub-experiment Farm. With the addition of the Northeast Experiment Station in Duluth in 1913, the Grand Rapids site became the North Central Experiment Station.

University of Minnesota Agricultural School

The School of Agriculture opened in 1926 and it became the North Central School of Agriculture. That began to phase out in 1963. The Duluth station closed in 1965 and by 1998 the Grand Rapids site became North Central Research and Outreach Center reflecting the changing roles of the facility and its programs.

Could it be possible that President Abraham Lincoln played a role in the establishment of an "Ag School" in Itasca County? Well, in point of fact, in 1862 he signed the Morrill Land-Grant Act paving the way for states to set up institutions of higher learning dedicated to such pursuits as mechanics or agriculture.

Itasca Junior College became Itasca State Junior College in 1964. Then a 1973 Minnesota legislative action changed the name of Itasca State Junior College to Itasca Community College (ICC). In 1985 ICC purchased five acres from the North Central Experiment Station to put in student housing. Other land was then leased to USDA Forest Experimental Station as well as ICC.

North Central Agricultural School Farm

From over 100 Gas Stations in Itasca County in the 1960's to under 30 in 2016

Lists

J.P. SIMS AND HIS PRIZE DRIVING TEAM AT ITASCA LBR Co CAMP NEAR SWAN LAKE

ITASCA COUNTY POST OFFICES

The Second Continental Congress began considering a postal system in the spring of 1775 for the conveyance of letters and intelligence between the Congress and the armies following the battles of Lexington and Concord. In the summer of 1776 Benjamin Franklin served as Postmaster General of the United States and the present Postal Service descends from the system Franklin put into operation.

Postal service for rural areas in the late 19th and early 20th century was still interesting, to say the least.

In Itasca County you will find the name of a post office without any documentation of where it was located. Examples include Kesahgah, which ran in 1857; Winnibigoshish, operating for three years beginning in 1905; and Arrow running from 1903 to 1906.

Another odd occurrence was the authorization of post offices which went so far as to register a name but were never actually established. The Busti Post Office was authorized in 1915; the Okoll and LaCroix offices, both authorized in 1907; and Irene authorized in1905. None of these were ever opened.

One post office, Compton, operating in Bass Brook township from 1891-92 merged with Cohasset.

Another office, Nass, serving Carpenter Township from 1913-1938 was relocated to that location from Celina in St. Louis County.

Bridgie Post Office operated in Nore Township from 1895-1908 when it became the Orth Post Office and continued operation until 1930.

From 1912-1933 the Leech Lake Indian Reservation had its own post office at Pinecrest.

Originally a goodly number of post offices were housed, almost as an auxiliary service, in various establishments such as general stores or hotels, even in private homes, rather than dedicated buildings.

Wawina Post Office

WILDWOOD/SPLITHAND TOWNSHIPS

Wildwood Township, with nearly 200 residents, wasn't formally organized until 1989. That's not a typo. It was 1989.

Another township late to the party is Splithand which was organized in 1985.

Early on, the tight knit farming community made good use of the fishing lakes in the area. George Moody developed his place into the first resort in 1904.

Others concentrated on potato farming or raising dairy cattle. These folks formed a chapter of Producers Market Association which was the predecessor of the Farm Bureau.

Splithand Township has had five different schools over the years, with the first named school being Cowhorn School in 1902. None of these exist anymore.

Blandin Paper Company owns one half of the land in Wildwood Township. Roughly one quarter of Splithand Township is also owned by Blandin Paper Company while another quarter of Splithand is Itasca County tax forfeited land. All these lands offer access to the public for recreation and hunting.

Cowhorn School at Splithand

Wildwood Township Hall

Old Cowhorn School

Farming in Splithand circa 1975

BALL CLUB

There are unique locations within the county that have a great significance beyond what is obvious.

The unincorporated community of Ball Club is certainly one of those.

Its largely Native American population of the Leech Lake Band of Ojibwe find themselves living within the Leech Lake Indian Reservation and the Chippewa National Forest.

The culture and traditions of the indigenous people remain intact with authentic celebrations, ceremonies, and festivals at the powwow grounds.

Ball Club lies on the border of Itasca and Cass counties.

Sitting at the south end of Ball Club Lake, the community was once a railway village with a designated post office.

Today one of its important roles is as a census-designated place (CDP). Simply explained, a CDP is a place of concentrated population identified by the United States Census Bureau for statistical purposes.

Every ten years a census is taken in this area as a counterpart of incorporated towns or cities. These statistics give important information about diversity, households and economics that might otherwise be missed.

Ball Club Lake has a shape resembling the bat used in an Indian game the French called La Crosse, hence its name and that of the community.

Providing its residents with a clinic, community center, as well as social services and education, Ball Club continues to be a unique location of significance in Itasca County.

Canoe at Ball Club

Ball Club Pow Wow

Indian Reservation ceremony

LEECH LAKE INDIAN RESERVATION

Linguistics matter in a discussion of the Indian people of Itasca County. Understanding the words makes a difference; especially when the history is researched and/or told by a white man.

Only two Indian Reservations are located, in part, in Itasca County. One of them holds great significance within the Minnesota Chippewa Tribe.

The Indian Reorganization Act of 1934 merged Leech Lake, Cass Lake, & Lake Winnibigoshish reservations of the Pillager Band along with the Chippewa Indian Reservation of Lake Superior Band and White Oak Point Reservation of the Mississippi Band of Chippewa to form the present "Greater Leech Lake Indian Reservation". The reservation, which is the largest in total area in Minnesota, enters portions of Itasca, Cass, Beltrami, and Hubbard counties. It also registers as the largest Indian Reservation in the state by total number of residents.

Watching the ceremony

While Itasca County houses most of the communities on Leech Lake Reservation, the largest community of Cass Lake is located in Cass County and is the site of Leech Lake Tribal Government.

The fact that nearly all of the reservation land is situated in the Chippewa National Forest enhances the reverence with which the Indigenous People hold the "Earth Mother". Their respect for the land and water that is their Native heritage continues to be taught to each new generation. And, in fact, the Chippewa language is part of the curriculum in many reservation schools and colleges.

Ceremonial Dancing

BOIS FORTE

Most Itasca County residents are aware of the existence and location of the Leech Lake Indian Reservation which begins near Deer River.

However, not all realize that the Bois Forte Reservation also locates in extreme northern Itasca County.

If a land is not inhabited by any Band members, is it still part of a reservation? Yes, because the Deer Creek section of Bois Forte was established by treaty in 1866. It belongs to the Bois Forte Band of Ojibwe also known as Chippewa.

The reservation is divided into three sectors. While no Band members reside in the Itasca County Deer Creek section, the section around Nett Lake in St. Louis County is home to the majority of Bois Forte Band members. It is said to be the largest producer of wild rice in the nation.

The Vermillion sector, near Tower in St. Louis County, is home to Fortune Bay Resort and Casino which opened in 1986. It employs more than 500 people and provides over $30 million to the northern Minnesota economy.

Bois Forte, meaning "strong wood", is governed by the Bois Forte Reservation Tribal Council.

Wild Rice Season

IJC/ICC/AG SCHOOL

It would have been impossible for one location in the State of Minnesota to offer all the features used in the state's vast agricultural endeavors. For that reason, the Minnesota Agricultural Experiment Station, established in 1885, requested and was granted, funds via a Minnesota legislative bill to operate two branch experiment stations. One was begun in Crookston in 1895 and named the Northwest Experiment Station and the second started in Grand Rapids in 1896 and was known as the Northeast Sub-experiment Farm. With the addition of the Northeast Experiment Station in Duluth in 1913, the Grand Rapids site became the North Central Experiment Station.

University of Minnesota Agricultural School

The School of Agriculture opened in 1926 and it became the North Central School of Agriculture. That began to phase out in 1963. The Duluth station closed in 1965 and by 1998 the Grand Rapids site became North Central Research and Outreach Center reflecting the changing roles of the facility and its programs.

Could it be possible that President Abraham Lincoln played a role in the establishment of an "Ag School" in Itasca County? Well, in point of fact, in 1862 he signed the Morrill Land-Grant Act paving the way for states to set up institutions of higher learning dedicated to such pursuits as mechanics or agriculture.

Itasca Junior College became Itasca State Junior College in 1964. Then a 1973 Minnesota legislative action changed the name of Itasca State Junior College to Itasca Community College (ICC). In 1985 ICC purchased five acres from the North Central Experiment Station to put in student housing. Other land was then leased to USDA Forest Experimental Station as well as ICC.

North Central Agricultural School Farm

From over 100 Gas Stations in Itasca County in the 1960's to under 30 in 2016

Lists

J.P. SIMS AND HIS PRIZE DRIVING TEAM AT ITASCA LBR Co CAMP NEAR SWAN LAKE

ITASCA COUNTY POST OFFICES

The Second Continental Congress began considering a postal system in the spring of 1775 for the conveyance of letters and intelligence between the Congress and the armies following the battles of Lexington and Concord. In the summer of 1776 Benjamin Franklin served as Postmaster General of the United States and the present Postal Service descends from the system Franklin put into operation.

Postal service for rural areas in the late 19th and early 20th century was still interesting, to say the least.

In Itasca County you will find the name of a post office without any documentation of where it was located. Examples include Kesahgah, which ran in 1857; Winnibigoshish, operating for three years beginning in 1905; and Arrow running from 1903 to 1906.

Another odd occurrence was the authorization of post offices which went so far as to register a name but were never actually established. The Busti Post Office was authorized in 1915; the Okoll and LaCroix offices, both authorized in 1907; and Irene authorized in1905. None of these were ever opened.

One post office, Compton, operating in Bass Brook township from 1891-92 merged with Cohasset.

Another office, Nass, serving Carpenter Township from 1913-1938 was relocated to that location from Celina in St. Louis County.

Bridgie Post Office operated in Nore Township from 1895-1908 when it became the Orth Post Office and continued operation until 1930.

From 1912-1933 the Leech Lake Indian Reservation had its own post office at Pinecrest.

Originally a goodly number of post offices were housed, almost as an auxiliary service, in various establishments such as general stores or hotels, even in private homes, rather than dedicated buildings.

Wawina Post Office

LNF = Location Not Found

AFFLECK = 1916-17   7 miles N of Grand Rapids in Arbo twp
ALVWOOD
ARROW = 1903-06   LNF
BALL CLUB
BASS LAKE
BEAUTY LAKE = authorized 1900 but never established
BEDE = 1903-06   LNF
BERGVILLE = 1904-35 in Ardenhurst twp
BIGFORK
BIRCHGROVE = 1912-13   LNF
BLACKBERRY
BOVEY
BOWSTRING
BUSTI = authorized 1915 but not established
CALUMET
COFFEY = 1911-19   10 miles NW of Deer River
COHASSET
COLERAINE
COMPTON = 1891-92   Bass Brook twp – merged with Cohasset
COOLEY = 1925-54
CORT = 1908-09   Greenway twp
CUNNINGHAM = 1901-13   Ardenhurst twp
DEER RIVER
DORA LAKE
DUNBAR = 1913-33 Good Hope twp
EFFIE
EVERGREEN = 1908-17 Bigfork twp
GOODLAND
GRAND RAPIDS
GREENROCK = authorized 1904 but not established - in Bearville twp

Keewatin Post Office
(Formerly Municipal Liquor Store)

Swan River Post Office

HOUPT = (AKA) Haupt) 1903-14 in Nore twp
INGER
JESSIE LAKE
KEEWATIN
KESAHGAH = 1857   LNF
LaCROIX = authorized 1907 but not established   LNF
LaPRAIRIE
LEIPOLD
MARBLE
MARCELL
MAX = 1906
MOOSE POINT
NASHWAUK
NASS = 1913-38 (transferred to this location from
    Celina in St. Louis Cty) in Carpenter twp
OKOLL = authorized 1907 but not established   LNF
ORCHID = 1905-27 Kinghurst twp
ORTH = 1908-30 in Nore twp was formerly at Bridgie 1895-1908
OSLUND = 1922-33 in Max twp
PENGILLY
PINECREST = 1912-33 in Leech Lake Reservation
PINEWOOD = 1903 LNF
RELEASE = 1908-12 in Balsam twp
ROSY = 1901-35
SPLITHAND = 1898-99 Unorganized Territory of South Itasca
SQUAW LAKE
SUOMI
SWAN RIVER

TACONITE
TALMOON
TOGO
TOLLEF = authorized 1902   LNF
VANCE = 1899-1901in Kinghurst twp ("Irene"
    1905 authorized but not established)
WABANA LAKE
WABANA
WARBA
WAWINA
WINNIBIGOSHISH = 1905-08   LNF
WIRT

Grand Rapids Post Office circa 1960

ITASCA COUNTY LAKES

Minnesota's state motto is "Land of 10,000 Lakes". Ten percent of those lie in Itasca County with names like Beauty, Blind Pete, Dirty Mike, Telephone and Little Inky. Depending on the year you count the named lakes, the number can vary, as evidenced by the life of Miller Lake in the Suomi Hills area. Miller Lake was one of numerous small lakes dotting the Suomi Hills Recreation Area fourteen miles north of Grand Rapids. In the summer of 1993 the beaver dam at the lake gave way creating a twelve-foot waterfall that sent the water cascading into Amen Lake below.

Before it cut a 70-foot deep washout, the waters of Miller Lake had covered twenty acres.

The Suomi area, to this day, is a hub for logging---mostly by beaver. These industrious creatures have an instinct to dam any waters they consider useable. That's what they did at Miller Lake. Whether it was the eroding of sandy subsoil beneath or the built up pressure on a weak spot in the dam that caused the thunderous cascade of water, Miller Lake became a puddle.

There seems to be a consensus that the natural loggers will not rebuild the dam. Then again, they did it once before. In 1982 their dam at the same location broke apart resulting in the building of a new dam at Miller Lake that gave way, again, in 1993!

Mary Shideler, known as the Kayak Lady, has paddled more than 825 named lakes in Itasca County, including Amen. But Miller Lake, for her, was a washout, so to speak.

The most common lake name in Itasca County is 'Bass', with a total of nine so named; followed by Long and Spring with eight each known by those names. There are almost eighty named lakes that begin with 'Little', from Little Antler to Little Wolf.

NAMED LAKES of ITASCA COUNTY

Adele
Alder Pone
Alex
Alice (Erwin)
Alice – Co Rd 33
Allen
Alp
Amen
Ames
Amic
Anderson
Ann
Antler
Arbo
Arrowhead – Hwy 6
Arrowhead – Co Rd 49
Aspen
Austin
Baldy
Balfour
Ball Club
Balloon (Barney)
Balsam
Barcus
Barness
Barrett
Bartlett
Barwise
Bass – Cohasset
Bass – Co Rd 336
Bass – Co Rd 69
Bass – Co Rd 310
Bass – Co Rd 21
Bass – Co Rd 340

Bass – Co Rd 29
Bass – Co Rd 4
Bass – Hwy 1
Batson
Battle
Bay—Co Rd 19
Bay—Co Rd 31
Bear
Beatrice
Beauty
Beaver – Hwy 38
Beaver – Co Rd 254
Beaver – Antler Lake
Beaver – Raddison Lake
Beaver – Co Rd 4
Beaver – Co Rd 49
Beaver – Orange Lake Rd
Beavertail
Becker
Bee Cee
Bello
Bengal
Bergville
Bevo
Biauswah
Big Balsam
Big Calf
Big Constance
Big Diamond
Big Dick
Big Green
Big Horn
Big Inky
Big Island
Big Jack
Big Jessie Pit
Big Too Much
Billo
Bills
Birch – Scenic Hwy 7
Birch – Co Rd 49
Birdseye
Black Island
Blackberry
Blackwater
Blandin (Sylvan)
Blandin (White Porky Lake)
Blind
Blind Pete
Bloom
Blue Rock – Northome
Blue Rock – Co Rd 49
Bluebill – Co Rd 345
Bluebill – Hwy 38
Bluewater
Bobby
Bog – Winnibigoshish

Bog – Burrows Lake
Bog – Hwy 2
Boggy
Boiler
Bosley
Bower
Bowstring
Bowstring Airport
Boy
Bray
Brown – Co Rd 45
Brown – Burrows Lake
Brush
Brush Shanty
Bryne
Buck – Hwy 38
Buck – Scenic Hwy 7
Buck -- Hwy 1
Buckeye Pit
Buckman
Bug
Buhella
Bullhead – Warba
Bullhead – Co Rd 256
Burns
Burnt Shanty
Burr
Burrows
Bustie
Busties
Butterfinger
Buttonbox
Cad
Callahan

Cameron
Camerton
Camp Five
Candy
Canoe
Captain Luke
Cappeletti
Caribou
Carlson
Caroline
Carpenter
Carpics
Cavanaugh
Cedar – Scenic Hwy 7
Cedar – Co Rd 4
Cemetery
Charlie
Charlotte
Chase
Chickadee
Christmas
Clarke
Clear
Clearwater – Co Rd 71
Clearwater – Co Rd 60
Clover Leaf
Clubhouse
Coddington
Coffee
Coca Cola
Coler
Coleman
Conners
Cook
Coon – Scenic State Park
Coon – Hwy 1
Copenhagen
Coppersmith

Cottonwood
Courtney
Cowhorn
Cranberry
Crane
Crescent
Crippled Deer
Crooked – Co Rd 427
Crooked – Co Rd 8
Crooked – Co Rd 49
Crooked – Co Rd 29
Cropless
Crum
Culp
Cut Foot Souix
Cutaway
Cutoff
Dalton
Damon
David
Day – Hwy 38
Day –Trout Lake
Dead Horse – Co Rd 17
Dead Horse – Co Rd 243
Dead Horse – Hwy 38
Decker
Deer – at Winnibigoshish
Deer – Co Rd 256
Deer – Hwy 1
Dethloff Slough
Dinner Pail
Dipper
Dirty Mike
Dishpan
Dixon

Doam (Four Boy)
Doan
Dock
Doctor
Dode
Doe – Co Rd 45
Doe – Hwy 38
Dogfish
Dollar
Dora
Draper Pit
Dry Creek
Duck – Co Rd 254
Duck – Co Rd 49
Duck – Hwy 1
Dunbar
Dunning
Eagle
East – Clubhouse Lake
East – Co Rd 29
East Smith
Edd
Edmund
Eel
Egg – Co Rd 37
Egg – Marcell
Eino
Elbow – Co Rd 525
Elbow – Co Rd 43
Elbow – Co Rd 35
Elizabeth
Elm
English
Erickson
Erskine
Ethel
Eve
Farley Lakes
Fawn
Figure Eight
Finley
Finn
First River
Fisher
Fishhook
Fiske
Five Island
Fly
Foley (Tuber)
Foot
Forest – Grand Rapids
Forest – Marcell
Forjer
Forsythe
Four Town
Fourth Sucker
Fox (Lemen/Roebuck)
Fox – Co Rd 45
Frances
Gabe

104

Garth
George – Co Rd 14
George – Co Rd 354
Georges
Ghost
Glove
Goodman
Goose
Grass – Co Rd 56
Grass – Co Rd 229
Grass – Hwy 38
Grassy
Grave
Greely
Green
Greenway
Guile
Gunderson
Gunn
Gunny Sack
Hale – Grand Rapids
Hale – Co Rd 67
Hale – Winnibigoshish
Half Moon
Hamrey
Hanson – Co Rd 59
Hanson – Co Rd 160
Harrigan
Harrison
Hart
Hartley
Haskell
Hatch
Hattie
Hawkins Pit
Hay – Co Rd 16
Hay – Co Rd 49
Heinen
Helen
Henrichs
Hendrickson
Hennessey
Herrigan
Herron
Highland
Hill
Hole-in-Wall
Holland
Holloway
Holman Pit
Holmes
Homestead
Hooligan
Hope
Horsehead – Co Rd 52
Horsehead – Co Rd 538
Horseshoe – Co Rd 355
Horseshoe – Kooch Co Line
Horseshoe – Co Rd 325
Horseshoe – Grand Rapids

Horseshoe – Hwy 38
Hudson
Hunters
Ice (Crystal)
Irene
Irma
Isaac – Scenic Hwy 7
Isaac – Scenic State Park
Island – Co Rd 525
Island – Co Rd 434
Island – Scenic Hwy 7
Island – Co Rd 60
Island – Northome
Island – Co Rd 48
Jack
Jack The Horse
Jaques
Jay Gould
Jean
Jessie
Jingo
Joe Fell
Joel
Johnson – Co Rd 539
Johnson – Beatrice
Johnson – Jack The Horse Lake
Johnson – Hwy 38
Jones
Joy
Judy's Lake
Kelly
Kennedy
Kenogama
Killdeer
King
Klingenpiel
Kremer
LaBarge
Lac La Boujou
Lac-A-Roy
LaCroix
Lake Fifty-Five
Lake of the Isles
Lake on Five
Lake Seventeen
Lake Twenty-Four
Lammon Aid
Larson
Larue Pit
Lauchoh
Lawrence – Scenic Hwy 7
Lawrence – Hwy 38
Layden
LeBarge

Lee
Leighton
Libby
Lillian
Lily – Co Rd 49
Lily – Hwy 1
Lily – Grand Rapids Airport
Lincoln
Linden
Little Antler
Little Arm
Little Ball Club
Little Bass – Cohasset
Little Bass – Marcell
Little Bear – Suomi
Little Bear – Co Rd 52
Little Birch
Little Blandin
Little Bowstring

Little Buck
Little Burnt Shanty
Little Calf
Little Clubhouse
Little Coon
Little Cottonwood
Little Cowhorn
Little Cut Foot
Little Dead Horse
Little Deer
Little Dew
Little Diamond
Little Dick
Little Dixon
Little Drum
Little East
Little Fowler
Little Horn
Little Horseshoe

Little Inky
Little Island – Hwy 1
Little Island – Co Rd 49
Little Island – Co Rd 16
Little Jay Gould
Little Jessie
Little Jessie Pit
Little Leighton
Little Long – Hwy 38
Little Long – Goodland
Little McCarthy
Little McKewen
Little Moose – Co Rd 551
Little Moose – Co Rd 238
Little Moose – Northome
Little Moose – Hwy 65
Little Moran
Little Mud
Little Neck

Little North Star
Little O'Brien
Little O'Reilly
Little Ole
Little Otter
Little Peterson
Little Porky
Little Rainbarrel
Little Ranier
Little Rice
Little Rose
Little Round
Little Ruby
Little Sand – Co Rd 4
Little Sand – Co Rd 70
Little Siseebakwet
Little Smith

Little South Fork
Little Splithand
Little Spring
Little Sturgeon
Little Sucker
Little Too Much
Little Trout
Little Turtle
Little Wabana
Little Wasson
Little White Oak
Little Whitefish
Little Winnibigoshish
Little Wolf – Co Rd 49
Little Wolf – Hwy 38
Logging Sleigh
Long – Co Rd 70
Long – Scenic Hwy 7
Long – Hwy 6
Long – Hwy 46

Long – Goodland
Long – Co Rd 63
Long – Co Rd 52
Long – Co Rd 19
Long Rainbarrel
Loon – Co Rd 256
Loon – Co Rd 69
Loon – Co Rd 63
Lorraine – Co Rd 562
Lorraine – Co Rd 533
Lost – Cohasset
Lost – Togo
Lost – Co Rd 52
Lost – Co Rd 33
Lost Moose
Lower Balsam
Lower Hanson
Lower Lawrence
Lower Panaca
Lower Pigeon
Lower Prairie
Lower Spring
Lower Twin East
Lower Twin West
Lucky
Lum
Lunden
Lynx
Maki
Mallard
Maple – Hwy 169
Maple – Co Rd 43
Marble
Marie – Scenic Hwy 7
Marie – Beltrami Co Line
Marlyn
Mary – Co Rd 45
Mary – Goodland
Matson
May
McAlpine
McAvity
McCarthy
McDonald – Co Rd 48
McDonald – Co Rd 254
McGrady
McGuire
McKewen
McKinley
McKinney
McVain
Mead
Middle Hanson
Middle Pigeon
Migary
Mike
Mikes
Miller
Mini Car Car
Minisogama
Mike
Minnow – Co Rd 49

106

Minnow – Winnibigoshish
Minny
Mirror
Mississippi
Mitt
Mole
Monson
Moon
Moonshine – Co Rd 49
Moonshine – Scenic Hwy 7
Moonshine – Co Rd 62
Moore
Moose – Nashwauk
Moose – Co Rd 58
Moose – Co Rd 19
Moose – Northome
Moose – Co Rd 333
Moose – Co Rd 12
Moose – Hay Creek
Moosetrack
Moran Morph
Mosomo
Moss
Mountain Ash
Mud
Mud – Co Rd 21
Mud – Calumet
Mud – Splithand
Mud – Suomi
Mud – Spang
Mulligan's Slough
Munzer
Murphy
Mushgee
Muskeg
Muskrat
My
Mystery
Nagel
Nameless
Napoleon
Nesseth

Nickel
No Mans
Noma
North Ackerman
North Star
Northome
Nose
O'Brien
O'Donnell
O'Leary
O'Reilly
Oak
Oar
Ole
One Loaf
Orange
Otter – Co Rd 52
Otter – Co Rd 246
Otter – Co Rd 533
Otter – Hwy 38
Owen
Oxhide

Pancake
Park
Pear – Hwy 169
Pear – Hwy 38
Peat
Pelton
Perch
Peterson
Pickerel – Co Rd 49
Pickerel – Orange Lake Rd
Pickerel – Hwy 6
Pickerel – Hwy 65
Pickerel – Wabana
Pickerel – Hwy 169
Pickerel – Co Rd 533
Pickle
Pigeon Dam
Pike – Co Rd 253
Pike – Goodland
Pine – Co Rd 45
Pine – Scenic State Park
Plantation
Plum
Pokegama
Poplar
Portage
Post
Potato – Co Rd 49
Potato – Hwy 11
Pothole
Poverty
Prairie – Scenic Hwy 7
Prairie – Co Rd 61
Pughole – Hwy 38
Pughole – Co Rd 45
Pughole – Co Rd 533
Pump
Rabbits
Raddison
Raft
Rahkos
Rainbarrel

Rainbow
Ralph's
Ranier
Raspberry
Rat – Co Rd 52
Rat – Hwy 1
Raven
Rearing Pond
Red
Reed Rice – Suomi
Rice – Co Rd 4
Rice – Hwy 38
Rice – Hwy 2
Rice – Beltrami Co Line
Rice – Cohasset
Rice Lake
Rip
Roberts
Rock – Co Rd 6
Rock – St. Louis Co Line
Roland
Roothouse
Rose
Rosholt
Rosy
Round – Co Rd 40
Round – Co Rd 71
Round – Goodland
Round – Co Rd 52
Round – Co Rd 46
Ruby
Rum
Rush Island
Ryan
Salter Pond
Sampson
Sand – Co Rd 2
Sand – Co Rd 4
Sand – Co Rd 49
Sawyer
Schoolhouse – Co Rd 126
Schoolhouse – Co Rd 46
Scooty
Scrapper – Co Rd 50
Scrapper – Co Rd 52
Seaman
Second
Section
Shafer
Shallow
Shallow Pond
Shamrock
Shelly
Sherry
Shine
Shingle Mill
Shoal – Hwy 38
Shoal – Co Rd 532
Shorty
Silver
Simpson
Sioux
Siseebakwet
Skeeter
Skelly
Skimerhorn
Slauson
Smith – Hwy 169
Smith – Co Rd 49
Snaptail
Snow
Snowball
Snowshoe
Someman
South Akerman
South Fork
South Smith
South Sturgeon
South Sugar
Spider
Spike
Splithand
Spot
Spring – Co Rd 525
Spring – Co Rd 29
Spring – Co Rd 69
Spring – Hwy 1
Spring – Co Rd 60
Spring – Cass Co Line
Spring at Cutaway Lake
Spring – Hwy 65
Spruce – Co Rd 474
Spruce – Co Rd 45
Spruce – Wabana
Spruce – Wirt
Spruce Island
Spur
Squaw
Steel
Stella
Stevens – Co Rd 62
Stevens – Co Rd 240
Stingy
Stokey
Stone Ax
Stowe
Stumple – Co Rd 45
Stumple – Co Rd 53
Sturgeon
Sucker – Co Rd 58
Sucker – Co Rd 1
Sugar
Sun
Sunken
Sunrise
Suomi
Surprise
Swan
Tadpole
Tamarack
Tank
Taylor
Telephone
Tell
The Pughole
Thimble
Third Sucker
Thirty
Thirtyone
Thistledew
Three Island
Three Island – Co Rd 45
Thyden
Tibbet
Tioga Pit
Tower
Trestle – Wirt
Trestle – Co Rd 56
Trible
Trout – Coleraine
Trout – Wabana
Tubby
Turtle
Tuttle
Twin – Co Rd 49
Twin – Marble
Twin – Hwy 6
Twin – Goodland
Two Island
Two Mile
Tye
Upper Hanson
Upper Hatch
Upper Panaca
Upper Pigeon
Upper Spring
Upper Twin
Van Patter
Virgin
Wabana
Wagner
Walters
Wamp
Warburg
Wart
Washington
Wasson
Weasel
Welch
West Smith
West Sturgeon
Whiskey
White Oak
White Porky
White Swan
Whitefish
Wilderness
Wileys
William
Williams
Willis
Willow
Wilson – Co Rd 51
Wilson – Klingenpiel Lk
Winnbigoshish
Wirt
Wolf – Hwy 38
Wolf – Co Rd 53
Your
Zimmy

108

Itasca County Civilian Conservation Corps (CCC)

F-14	Cutfoot Sioux	707
F-15	Winnibigoshish	708
F-26	Sand Lake	706
F-27	Inger	1797
F-32	Mack	1724
F-34	Day Lake	786
F-35	Stokes	1714
F-36	Squaw Lake	1762
F-37	Wirt	4709
F-45	Thirteen Mile	
F-51	Wagner Lake	2701
S-54	Owen Lake	718
S-59	Third River	1761
S-95	Deer Lake (Effie)	3711
SP-3	Scenic State Park	1722

ITASCA COUNTY TRAIN STATIONS

Would you ever call a train or railroad "goofy"? You might after you hear this story.

The Duluth & Winnipeg Railway reached Grand Rapids by 1890 and then went on to Deer River. But timber men were pressing for a logging railroad so construction of the Itasca Railroad started in Cohasset. There, difficulties with land use agreements and financial reimbursements forced the company to pull up the rails and relocate west to Deer River in

Bovey Train Station

"Gut & Liver"

1893. The Itasca Railroad property was transformed in 1901 into the Minneapolis & Rainy River Railroad (M&RRR). That led to extending the rails north of Suomi with a branch line taking a northwest heading and terminating in Wirt.

An old map shows no fewer than 35 whistle stops along the M&RRR. It's said that for that reason the train didn't stop for anything else including cows and wildlife. And that's how the M&RRR got the nickname of "The Gut & Liver", so the story goes. It hit so many animals that the cow catcher at the front of the train was covered with the remains.

There's a second explanation for the nickname that refers to its service to logging camps.

The M&RRR delivered supplies to the outlying camps, and since there was no refrigeration, most of the meats delivered were sausage (guts) and liver.

If not goofy, it's at least unique. Oh, and Minneapolis & Rainy River Railway never reached either of the locations it was named for.

Swan River Train Station

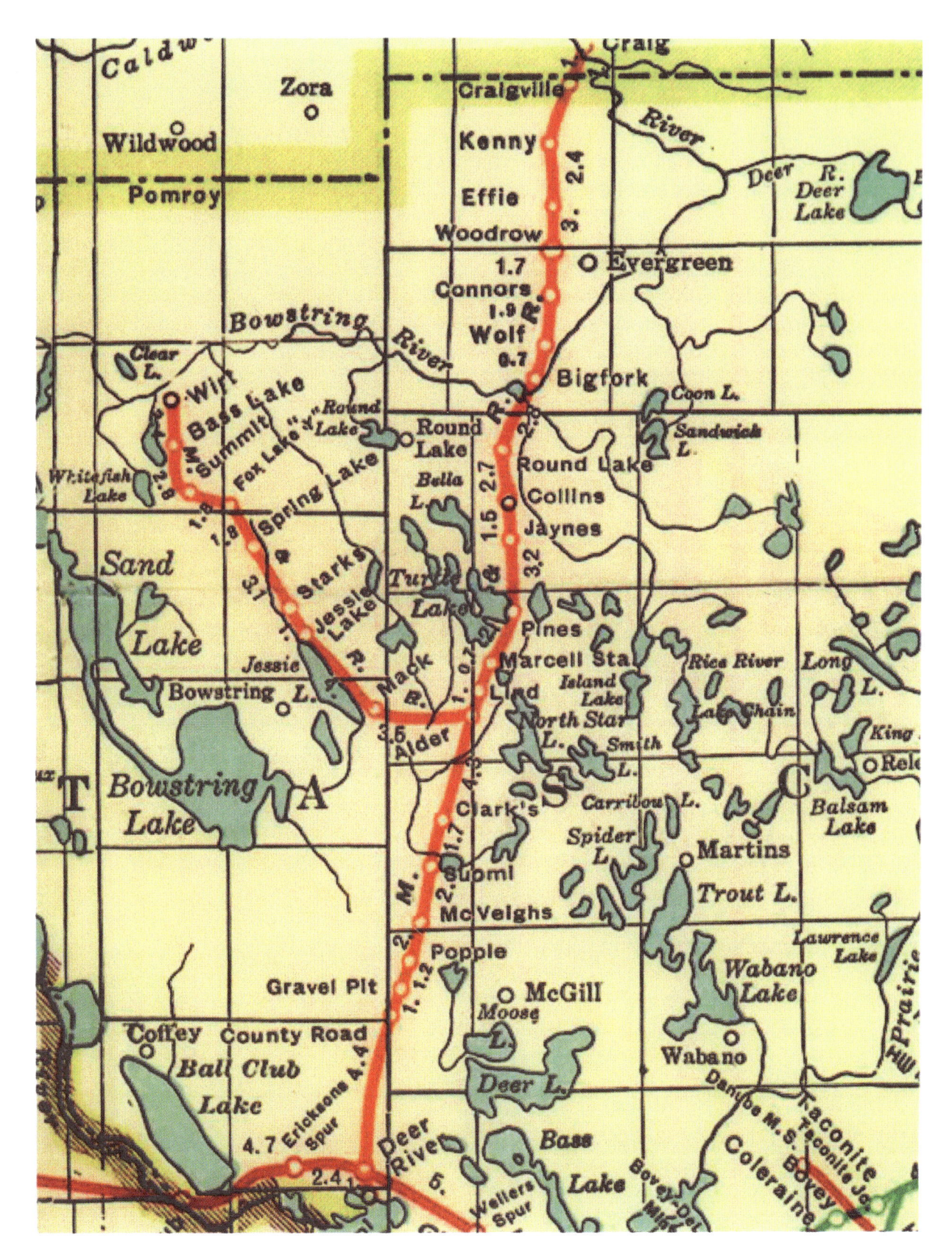

Whistle stops on the "Gut & Liver" Rail line

ACROPOLIS = in Goodland Township - Great Northern Railway

ALDER = Marcell Township on Minneapolis & Rainy River Railroad (M&RRR)

ARCTURUS = Duluth, Missabe & Northern Railway (sect 24) Iron Range Township

BENGAL = Great Northern in Goodland Township

BENNETT = Great Northern in Nashwauk Township

BRIDGIE = Minnesota & International Railway in Cormorant Township; was transferred to Orth

BRUCE = Goodland Township on Great Northern route until 1940s when it became called 'Morrell'

CALYX = Duluth, Missabe &Northern Railway in Lone Pine Township

CANISTEO = Iron Range Township on Great Northern

COUNTY ROAD = Deer River Township of M&RRR ("Gut & Liver" railway)

DUMAS = Great Northern in Morse Township

ERICKSON = Great Northern in Morse Township

Wawina Train Station

Jesse Train Station

Alder transfer station

112

EVERGREEN = M&RRR

FOX LAKE = M&RRR in Wirt Township

GUNN = Great Northern in Grand Rapids Township

HOLMAN = in Iron Range Township on Duluth Missabe & Western also on Great Northern

HOUPT = (AKA Haupt) Minnesota & International Railway

JAYNES = M&RRR (Gut & Liver) in Stokes Township

KENNY = M&RRR in unorganized Territory of Effie

LIND = M&RRR in Marcell Township

MARCELL JUNCTION = M&RRR   2 miles S of Marcell

MAX = Great Northern

MCVEIGH= M&RRR in Deer River Township

MOORE = Great Northern in Nashwauk Township

MORRELL = Great Northern Goodland Township

NOYES = Duluth, Missabe & Iron Range Railroad in Lone Pine Township

ORTH = Northern Pacific Railroad

PINES = M&RRR in Marcell Township

ROSY = M&RRR in Third River Township

SAVANNAH = Duluth, Missabe & Northern

STARKS = M&RRR in Lake Jessie Township

SUMMIT = M&RRR in Wirt Township

TURTLE JUNCTION = M&RRR in Marcell Township

VAN CAMPS = M&RRR in Bigfork Township

WELLERS = (AKA Wellers Spur OR Weller's Spur) 5 miles SE of Deer River in Bass Lake Township

WHITE FISH LAKE = M&RRR in Wirt Township

WOLF = M&RRR in Bigfork Township

WYMAN = Duluth & Iron Range Railroad in Nashwauk Township

Deer River Train Depot

Cohasset Train Depot

Marcell Train Stop

ITASCA COUNTY MINES

Loggers had some advantages over miners in developing Itasca County. For one thing, trees grew back, but ore didn't. Once the art of conservation was embraced by loggers, they could replenish the forests, though it would take time.

Miners, on the other hand, extracted all they could from the rocks and with that supply depleted, the only thing to do was give up. Technology allowed for new and better means to get the most from the ore. It could not replace what had been taken.

Another advantage the loggers had was the fact that there were forests everywhere. Itasca County had only relatively small deposits of ore unlike the neighboring counties to the east.

Hundreds of mines sprang up in the early 1900s in Itasca County. Numerous mining companies rushed to exploit new found deposits. There are still valuable minerals lying beneath the tree covered ground, but recovering it may prove to be cost prohibitive and the mines of Itasca County may have seen their last hurrah.

Bovey:
- Danube
- Fletcher
- Holman Cliffs – Bingham
- Holman Cliffs – Brown
- Homestead – 068
- Judd
- Lewis
- Morrison
- N.W. I. Reserve St-1 & St-3
- Plummer
- Sally
- US Steel Reserve 0-69
- Walker

Calumet:
- Allen Rossum Reserve
- Butler Taconite Pit No. 5
- David Reserve Bu-2
- Draper
- Hanna Mining
- Hill Annex
- Langdon
- Majorca
- MN State of
- Patrick-Ann
- Rita Reserve
- Sargent Reserve

Men and Women miners in Keewatin

Mining Railroad repair vehicle

Scott Reserve
Snowball Reserve
Taconite Reserve

Cooley:
Ann
David
Harrison
Longdon
Patricke-Kevin
Butler Tac

Cohasset & Grand Rapids:
Beckfelt Reserve
Finnegan Reserve
Hanna Iron Ore
Hartman Reserve
Jordon Reserve
Marr Reserve
Salter Reserve
T Russell Estate
Tioga No 1
Tioga 2

Coleraine:
Buckeye
Buckeye Reserve
Canisteo
Fargo Reserve
Hummer
Jennison
Jessie #1 & #2
King
Lind-Greenway
West Hill

Marble:
Arcturus
Barbara
Delaware #1 & #2
GNIOP & Brooks Walker
Gross-Marble
Hanna
Hill Annex
Hill Trumbull-Potter
Hill Trumbull
J & L Hill Annex
Walker-Hill #4,#5,#6
Walker Hill Parcel 4&5

Keewatin:
Alexander
Aromac
Bennett

Canisteo Mercantile Co. in Bovey

Bennett Mine cook shack in Keewatin

Drilling equipment in Keewatin

Bray
Carlz
Cyprus
Forest
Gordon
Hanna Mining
Hunt
KeeTac – US Steel
Lamberton
Mace
Mahoning
Magnetation
Mesabi Chief
Mississippi
National Steel
National Tac –
   Hanna Mining
Perry
Russell
Sargent
Section 18
St. Paul
Stein
Stevenson
Wyman

Nashwauk:
   Argonne
   Butler Bros
   Butler Taconite
   Carol
   G-10
   Galbraith
   Halobe
   Hanna
   Harrison
   Hawkins
   Helen
   Hoadley
   Kevin
   LaRue
   Leach
   Mace
   Mackillican
   Midwest Reserve Bu-12
   O'Brien Reserve Bu-14
   Olson
   Patrick
   Patrick-Ann

Canisteo Mine loading train

Oliver Train in Bovey

Tioga Mine #2

116

        Quinn
        Shade
        Snyder
        Sullivan No.2
        Taconite Reserve Bu-10
        Vernon
        York

Taconite:
        Diamond
        Holman Cliffs – North Star

Trout Lake:
        Washing Plant near Trout Lake

Itasca County:
        Magnetation
        Essar Steel

Oliver Iron Mining Co. Train

La Rue Mine View

Holman Mine Scenic View

ITASCA COUNTY BARS AND SALOONS

This incomplete listing is but a sampling of the many places throughout the county where beer and liquor has been or is served. Many establishments in the early days were located in the owner's homes and may have lasted only a short time. Because ownership changed often, it is difficult to determine who started many of the taverns or bars or who all the owners were.

aka = also known as
fka = formerly known as
nka = now known as

4 Cedars …Co Rd 63, SW of Cohasset …A. T. Rupert
8 Mile Tavern #1…1960…8 mi S of GR at Matuska Road…four Harms brothers: Emil, Harry, Clarence, and ??
8 Mile Tavern #2…replaced #1 after a few months- built with material salvaged from courthouse demolition
17th Street Grill…144 SE 17th St, GR…Burl Ives
Alamo…403 NE 5th Ave, GR…Ann Stuckslager, Bernie Schedin…became Red Carpet in 70s…now it is Schroeder Family Dentistry
Allan's Resort…Co Rd 68 on Little Splithand Lake…Archie Allan…later became Aunt Nancy's
American Legion – McVeigh-Dunn Post #60… 1991…9 NW 2nd St, GR…previously at 120 NW 3rd St
American Legion Club – Post #452…Keewatin
Antler Lodge…on Antler Lake…51754 Scenic Hwy 7, Bigfork…Fred Bentz
Applebee's Neighborhood Grill & Bar…2840 Hwy 169, GR
Arbo Store & Tavern …7 mi N of GR on Hwy 38… built by Erling & Fran Willadson…Jalmar & Norma Lake, Gary & Jane Reinarz, Doyle Skallman…closed in 1988
Arcadia Lodge…on Big Turtle Lake…52001 Co Rd 284, Bigfork…established 1922 by Joe Cardarille… Les Sloat, Doug Eaton, Steve & Becky Jones
Arcana Hotel Bar…Coleraine
Arrowhead Café…1st Ave NW, between 2nd & 3rd St, GR…next to Costello's Ice Cream Parlor… Harvey Madson
Aunt Nancy's…Little Splithand Lake…see Allon's Resort
Avalon Dance Hall & Bar…W 4th St between 5th & 6th Ave, GR
B. Baaken's on the Beach…32946 Crystal Springs Rd, GR…Butch Baaken…nka Zorbas

118

Baker's Bar…1898
Ball Club Hotel & Saloon…Frank Payne
Beach's Store…8 mi N on Hwy 38…Bob & Angie Beach…1st store burned in 1942, 2nd store burned in 1959
Beaver Inn...Big Rice Lake SW of Cohasset…Slim Stark family
Bernie's Main Dry…216 N 1st St, Keewatin…Bernadine DeNucci
Bertha's...Cohasset…Bertha Ridlon…had a bar in the front room of her house
Big Dan's…Bovey…Dan Trboyevich…later became Viv's
Bigfork Wilderness Bar…Bigfork
Bill's Place…aka Sunset Tavern & Pee Hole Inn…1800 McKinney Lake Rd, GR…original owner: John Peterson
Black Cherry Liquors...5200 Hwy 169 S, GR…Dale Nichols…closed 2009
Blackberry Store...Hwy 2 E & Co Rd 71…Al Bengston, Leonard & Shirley Johnson, Fred Tanner
Blackwater Inn...Cohasset…old Hwy 6 at MP&L exit…Rodney & Mona Fuller
Blue Moon Tavern…Hwy 169 S across from 9 Mile Corner Tavern…Lloyd Erickson
Blueberry Bowl…Hwy 6 N & Golf Course Rd, DR…Tim & Harry Rasley
Bobbers Bar…43465 Williams Narrows Rd, DR
Bob's Bar & Restaurant...Hwy 2 in Cohasset…Bob & Sheila Deutsch…sold to MNDOT 2008
Bodega…McAlpine Bldg, GR…1892…John McDonald
Brewski's Bar & Grill…209 Alice St, Marble…nka Hannibal's Bar & Grill
Bridgeside Restaurant & Sport…32946 Crystal Springs Rd, GR…nka Zorbas
Burns' Saloon…pre 1900
Cabin City Tavern…4th St NE & 9th Ave, GR…Lottie Peterson, Dick Stensrud
Cal's Bar…Keewatin…Sue & Dave Stahlboerger
Camp Caribou…about 20 miles N on Hwy 38…Jack Halvorson, Jenny Burnison, Irene Wall
Cannata's…Keewatin
Cannibal Junction…Hwy 6 N of DR at junction Co Rd 35…nka Riley's Fine Food & Drink
Captain Hook's…32946 Crystal Springs Rd, GR…Chris Hookland…nka Zorbas
Casablanca...3 mi E of Hwy 169 on LaPlant Rd, GR...south side...M. P. & Lillian Parker…early to mid 1940s
Cassidy's Saloon…Taconite
Cedar Creek Grill…34769 N Hwy 38, GR…fka Wilderness Pub
Chicken Shack …..W 4th St, GR…aka McVeigh's…Bill Hoolihan, Chuck Rusnak

119

Chinese Dragon…220 NE 2nd Ave, GR…burned

Clark Smith Saloon & Tobacco Store…1890-1895…bought out by Thomas 'Pig Eye' Kelly in August 1899…John Boyle O'Reilly bought a half interest…name was changed to O'Reilly & Kelly saloon. O'Reilly bought Kelly out in June 1900.

Club 65…Pengilly…Pete Marinoff…

Cohasset Liquor Store…at the bridge in Cohasset…sold to Troop brothers who relocated to Hwy 2

Colonel's Place…Pengilly…1978…Jim Elmes …sold in 1996 & became a church

Corner Bar…Taconite…Toivo Saari, Red Hart, R. Rasmussen, E. Camilli, Berardo & Sigfrinius, Jim (Bud) & Judy Ryser, Ventrucci

Country House…32969 LaPlant Rd, GR …Jim Fierek, Ralph Olson…fka Point's Retreat…closed 2015

Cozy Inn…1950…410 NW 6th Ave, GR…Leo & Margaret St. Martin

Crazy Loon…16171 Half Circle Dr, Pengilly

Crow Bar & Grill…5748 St Hwy 46, Squaw Lake…nka Fish Tales 2014

Dale's Bar…502 Roosevelt St, Coleraine…Dale Nordin…became Firehouse Bar & Grill

Deer Lake Charlie's…66501 Co Rd 533, Effie

Diamond Bar…Coleraine…Tony Mehelich

Don's Hut…209 Alice St, Marble…Don & Alana Martella…nka Hannibal's Bar & Grill

Double "R" Bar…see Hawkie's Tavern

Double "T" Bar…Hwy 2, Cohasset…Charlie & Harold Troop

Dozer's Bar & Grill…16211 Half Circle Dr, Pengilly

Drumbeater Supper Club…1979…32946 Crystal Springs Rd, GR…Bob & Debbie Anderson…nka Zorbas

Dugout…aka Ozzie's…15 NW 2nd St, GR…Herb Gist & J. Ward Ozbun…Lawrence Hawkinson purchased from Herb Gist…now empty lot

Dutch Room…original in West Hotel…320 NW 3rd St, GR…Bill Hoolihan & Doug Beckwith, Wm. H. Litchke, Cliff Sommers, Denny Madden, Lawrence Hawkinson sold to BPC for wood yard

Eagles – Aerie #2469…1776 S Hwy 169, GR…previously at 13 NW 2nd St.

East End Tavern…322 NE 4th St, GR…Louis L. & Maggie (Gunn) Laurent, Art DeBellis…later Beno's Pizza, now is Dottie's Café

Ed Wellein's Pool Parlor…NW 3rd St, GR…next to Ratican Café…before 1930

Eldie's…1212 NW 4th St, GR…Eldie Allison…nka Toivo's

Firehouse Bar & Grill…Coleraine…fka Dale's Bar…closed
Fireside Inn…1900 McKinney Lake Rd, GR…George ("Black George") & Aldona Cehlar…became LaCocina
Fish Tales…50748 St Hwy 46, Squaw Lake…fka Crow Bar & Grill
Florio's Grill & Tavern…105 NW Main St, Cohasset
Forest Lake Lodge…1216 NW 5th St, GR…Gus Huhn, Vic Vikre, Duane & Marilyn Reno…burned 1964
Forest Lake Restaurant & Bar…1201 NW 4th St, GR…
Fourth Street Station…1212 NW 4th St, GR…see Eldie's
Fraser House…early LaPrairie…John Fraser, Toole & O'Connell 
Gentile's Beer Tavern…Keewatin…burned 1953
Glade #1…Cohasset…Hwy 2 W & Co Rd 128…formerly Bar X…John Skelly…burned
Glade #2…Hwy 169 E & 11th Ave, GR
Golden Spike Bar…Marble…Spike & Joni Eichorn…torn down
Gosh Dam Place…Hwy 46 & Co Rd 9, DR
Grow's 169 Club…Hwy 169 S, GR
Gulseth's Tavern…Old Hwy 169 midway between GR & Coleraine…Oral Gulseth
Hannibal's Bar & Grill…209 Alice St, Marble…fka Brewski's Bar & Grill
Happy Hollow…Blackberry…Hwy 2 East & Happy Hollow Rd…originally Chris Peterson's store 1940s…Bill Karna, Jerry Hoffman
Harbor…4 mi S on Hwy 169, GR…Lino Cechini, Grayce Cameron, Evie Terebayza…later became Savoy On The Lake
Harbor Grand Sports Bar & Grill…20184 US Hwy 169, GR..fna The Harbor
Harley's Hut…Marble…Harley Jensen…nka Hannibal's Bar & Grill
Hawkie's Tavern…River Rd, GR…1940-59…renamed Double "R" Bar…Kenneth Hawkinson
Hay Creek Lodge…Pengilly…Joe & Mary Baratto, Don & Margaret Roberts…became Mr. Roberts
Hayslip's Corner…Talmoon…D. H. Hoover, Leo Hayslip, Richard Shearen
Hepfel's Beer Garden…W 3rd St, GR…across street from Royal Bar…John Hepfel
Herr's Bar…Mishawaka Rd, GR…Pete Herr
Hi-Hat…Cohasset…Hwy 2 W & Hwy 6…Herb Gist & Leo Heddens…burned

Hotel Pokegama

Hotel Pokegama

Hill…51506 State Hwy 46, Squaw Lake…Bruce & Sandy Leino
Hi-Lo Lounge…202 NW 3rd St, GR…adjacent to Royal Bar
Hi-View…Hwy 169 S, GR…William C. Smith, Caryl & Mary Arnold
Hoot 'N Holler…Junction of Hwy 46 & Co Rd 13, Alvwood
Inkman's…Cloverdale…N of Nashwauk
Jam's Corner Bar…200 Central Ave, Nashwauk
Jay-Bee Inn…Pengilly…originally Judy's Café…John & Bernie Keck, Katy & Mac MacLaren, Georgia Sarich
Jim Sherry's Saloon…1890s…Blandin Mill site
Joe & Cleo's Tavern…410 NE 4th St, GR…Joe & Cleo Guerin
Joe Jones' Saloon…Bigfork…early 1900s
Johnson Brothers Hotel & Saloon…1891
Johnson's Recreation & Pool Hall…215 N Pokegama Ave, GR…Ham Johnson, formerly Quakenbush Saloon, then Ed Huson's Pool Hall…now Wells Fargo drive-up bank & parking
Junction Bar & Grill…Togo
Keoki Reef..1315 NE 7th St, GR…George & Joe Makedonsky…early 1960s….burned after 2 yrs
Kuschel's Tavern…210 NW 2nd St, GR…Fred Kuschel… became Mill Pond
LaCocina…1900 McKinney Lake Rd, GR…fka Fireside Inn
Lakes Inn…1300 E. US Hwy 169, GR…fka Rainbow
Lakeview Tavern…Co Rd 12 & Jefferson Ave, Pengilly…Louie & Ann DeLuca, Hoone DeLuca, Jim Peluso
Lawrence Lake Liquors…33887 Scenic Hwy 7, Bovey
Lazi Daz Stopover…28073 Splithand Rd, GR
Leino's Bar…Squaw Lake…Eino Leino
LMNO P-ZA & Uecker's Eat & Drinkery…W Hwy 2, GR
Locker Room…403 Roosevelt Ave, Coleraine…Ron Maki
Logan's Saloon…Keewatin…early 1900s
Loggers Bar & Grill…104 Hwy 38 S, Bigfork…burned
Lone Pine Saloon…Keewatin…early 1900s…Patrick McGuire
Long Lake Lodge…N Scenic Hwy 7 & Co Rd 52, Bigfork…burned
Lyons Hotel & Saloon…Ball Club…Frank Payne
Madden's Dutch Room & Mad Dog's Pizza…702 NW 4th St, GR…Denny Madden
Maple Grove Resort…Hwy 169 S, GR…Schultz, Lino Cechini…became Harbor
Mazzo's…Bovey
McCormick's Store...Hwy 38 N & Co Rd 233...Grace McCormick, Denny Yurick...sold to MNDOT
McVeigh's…1900 +…aka Chicken Shack
Midway Tavern…E Hwy 169 & Pear Lake Rd, GR…Roy Mattfield
Mike O'Toole Refreshments/Saloon…1890…SE 1st St & 5th Ave, GR
Mike's Bar…209 – 2nd St, Bovey…Mike & Gina Pavlica…sold to Mike Bibich who also bought Palm Garden & combined the two, still keeping the name Mike's Bar
Mill Pond…210 NW 2nd St, GR…Ozzie Ozbun, Leo Hedin, John Bymark, Sr,. Donnie Madson
Miner's West End Tavern & Grocery…1202 NW 4th St, GR…Tony Miner
Moose Lodge 2023…330 NE 10th Ave, GR
Mr. Roberts…28179 E Shore Dr, Pengilly…see Hay Creek Lodge
Mulligan's Restaurant & Pub…3910 Golf Course Rd, GR
Municipal Liquors…Marble…became Golden Spike Bar
Nap Varin's Bar…W 4th St, GR, just W of Anderson Glass

Nason's Day & Night Club…1887…NE Pokegama Ave, GR at present Blandin Foundation site
Neighborhood Tavern…Effie
Nine Mile Corner…Hwy 169 S & Co Rd 67…G. J. Baldwin, Matzdorf family was last owner…closed 2010
Nip & Sip…see Hi-Lo Lounge
North Star…early LaPrairie…J. H. McDonough
Nyhus Resort…West Bay Dr, Pengilly…Fred & Opal Nyhus…closed in 1957
Oasis…Hwy 2 E, LaPrairie…aka Village Inn and Silver Spur
Old Calumet Saloon…995 Gary St, Calumet…Dode & John Tulibaski
Old Municipal Liquor Store…Deer River…closed 1981
O'Leary & Fraser Saloon…early GR
O'Reilly & Kelly Saloon…..see Clark Smith Saloon
Outpost Bar & Grill…203 NW 4th Ave, DR
Owl's Nest…5 SW 10th St, GR
Ozzie's…see Dugout
Palm Garden…Bovey…Joe Shustarich, Dee Bluntach…sold to Mike Bibich
Palmer's Tavern…Pengilly…Mae Palmer, J. J. Hansen, Joe Barrato, Virginia Jam…became Penguin Club
Pattee's Store & Tavern…19473 Hwy 169 S, GR…John Pattee, Dean Peck, Bob Patterson, Ken Patterson…nka Pokegama Lake Store
Patterson's Store & Tavern…19473 Hwy 169 S, GR…Bob Patterson, Ken Patterson…fka Pattee's Store
Peck's Store & Tavern…19473 Hwy 169 S, GR…Dean Peck…fka Pattee's Store
Pee Hole Inn…1800 McKinney Lake Rd, GR…owned by lady named Peedy from California…aka Bill's Place and Sunset Tavern
Penguin Club…See Palmer's Tavern
Pla-Mor Club…Pengilly…John & Leola Yochum, Mike & Mildred Miskovich
Point's Retreat…32969 LaPlant Rd, GR…Uno & Ethel Point…became Country House
Pokegama Bar…220 N Pokegama Ave, GR…became Red Eye Saloon
Pokegama Lake Store…19473 Hwy 169S, GR…see Pattee's Store
Rainbow…1300 E US Hwy 169, GR…Lawrence Hawkinson; Leroy & Darlene Hawkinson; Otto Hauger; Dee & Tudy Motschenbacher; Cliff Nelson; Juan Lazo; Kevin McNichols…nka The Lakes Inn
Red Carpet…Rick Courtney & Al Curran…fka Alamo…closed late 70s
Red Rooster…GR…Hwy 38 N & Co Rd 60…Louie Lagerstrom…became a rock shop/antique store
Red Eye Saloon…220 N Pokegama Ave, GR…fka Pokegama Hotel Bar…burned 1974
Red Eye Saloon…14301 St Hwy 65, Swan River
Red Hart's Bar…N on Scenic Hwy, Bovey
Rendezvous…River Rd, GR…former Fear's Grocery & Feed Store (?)…Pat Taylor
Rendezvous…Hwy 169 E, GR across from Pepsi warehouse…Ben Aultman, Ray Schultz
Rendezvous 2...Golf Course Rd W of Pokegama Ave, GR...closed 2009
Richie's Marcell Inn & Supper Club…48644 St Hwy 38, Marcell
Riley's Fine Food & Drink…46551 Riley Rd, DR…fka Cannibal Junction
River Italian…208 NE 3rd St, GR…closed
Roadway…Calumet…Paul Preice, Earl Ridlon, Jerry Radakovich, Red Hart, Fred Tanner, Mike Bibich
Royal Bar & Hi-Lo Lounge…202 NW 3rd St, GR…aka Nip & Sip, Zoo

Royal Buffet…Apr 13, 1901…Kelly McDougal's new saloon, GR
Rub-A-Dub Bar…Pengilly…Georgia Sarich
Ryiney's…Mar 3, 1900…John Ryiney purchased Sayer Bldg on Leland Ave to open a saloon, GR…Jun 23, 1900…Ryiney sold saloon to Matt Schumacher
Savoy On The Lake…20184 US Hwy 169 S, GR…fka The Harbor
Saw Mill Inn…2302 S. Hwy 169, GR…fka Holiday Inn
Scenic Pines Bar & Grill…29314 Co Rd 52, Bigfork
Shadowland...Hwy 169 E, GR…near Prairie River bridge parking lot
Shady Rest…Hwy 46 & Co Rd 39, Ball Club
Shay's Family Restaurant & Lounge…Hwy 2, DR…Jim Shay
Sid Milaney's Card Room…1st Ave NW, GR…next to Arrowhead Cafe
Silver Spur…Hwy 2, LaPrairie…aka Village Inn and Oasis
Sugar Lodge…on Sugar Lake, GR…Art & Eleanor Otis…burned
Sunset Tavern…see Bill's Place & Pee Hole Inn
Supper Club…Ball Club…Cliff & Sue Sjolund, Cliff Jr & Agnes Sjolund, Jim & Loretta Harwood, Jack Heathman & Judy Horner
Ted & Vi's…1201 ½ NW 4th St, GR…Ted Lukehart
Thunderbird Bar…115 N 1st St, Keewatin
Timberwolf Inn…Hwy 38 N of Marcell
Tom Foolery's…1/2 mi S of Pokegama Lake bridge, GR…Jim MacNeil…burned
Town Pump...Cohasset
Tracey's On Main Bar & Grill…Marble…Tracey Schwartz…nka Hannibal's Bar & Grill
Troop Town Store…SE end of Pokegama Lake off Sunny Beach Road…Charlie Troop
Yukon...1st Ave NW, S of Cole's Hardware on 2nd St, GR…originally Ehrke's Grocery…displaced when Mornes built new store there in 1945
Vault 65…Nashwauk
Vene-Qua…201 N 1st St, Keewatin…Annette Gilbert
Verchota's Store…see Voltz's Store
Veteran's of Foreign Wars – Ponti-Peterson Post 1720…14 NW 3rd St, GR
Vet's Club...Deer River
Village Inn…1721 Hwy 2 E, LaPrairie…Dick Voges, Tony Hahne…aka Silver Spur and Oasis
Viv's Liquor…Bovey…Vivian Trboyevich…fka Big Dan's
Voight's Store & Tavern…Hwy 19, DR…Charlie Voight, Felix Ikola
Voltz's Store…S of Cohasset on Hwy 6…Emil Voltz…later became Verchota's Store…aka 13 Mile Corner
Wagon Wheel Bar…Deer River…Donnie Madson
Warba Liquor Store...Hwy 2, Warba…Wilcox family's first bank…Bill Basham
Wallein's Liquor…215 NW 1st Ave, GR…1936…Al Wallein
Wally's Ribs…Hwy 169 S, GR…1978
Wendigo Lodge Restaurant & Bar…20108 Golf Crest Dr, GR…closed
Wigwam…Witmas Hotel, Bovey…John Witmas…burned 1954
Wilderness Bar…Bigfork…Dan Infante & Darlene Westerman…aka Picaroon Saloon
Wilderness Pub…34579 N Hwy 38, GR…nka Cedar Creek Grill
Willow Beach…Ball Club…closed
Wizard's Bar & Grill…102 Central Ave, Nashwauk
Zorbas…32946 Crystal Springs Rd, GR…fka The Drumbeater, Captain Hook's, B. Baaken's on the Beach, Bridgeside

ITASCA COUNTY CHURCHES

Grand Rapids
Assembly of God Church
Baha'i Faith
Calvary Pines Baptist
Christ Episcopal
Christ Memorial Episcopal
Church of Christ
Church of Jesus Christ of
    Latter Day Saints
Church of the Nazarene
Community Presbyterian
Church of Good Shepard
Evangelical Free Church
Faith Baptist Church
Fellowship of Believers
First Evangelical Lutheran
First Church of God
First Church of Christ Scientist
Full Gospel Church
Grace Bible Chapel
Grand Rapids Alliance Church
Grand Rapids Assembly of God
Grand Rapids Baptist Church
GR Seventh Day Adventist Church
Jehovah's Witnesses
Reed Memorial Methodist
Restoration Life Church
Salem Lutheran Brethren
St. Andrew's Lutheran
St. Joseph's Catholic Church
St. Luke's Evangelical Lutheran Church
St. Patrick's Catholic
The Solid Rock Church of God
Unitarian Chapel
United Methodist
United Pentecostal
Zion Lutheran

Bigfork
Bigfork Assembly of God Church
First Presbyterian Church of Bigfork

Bovey
Bethel Lutheran Church
Bethel-Trinity Lutheran
Lawron Presbyterian
Mount Olive English Lutheran
Triumphant Life Church

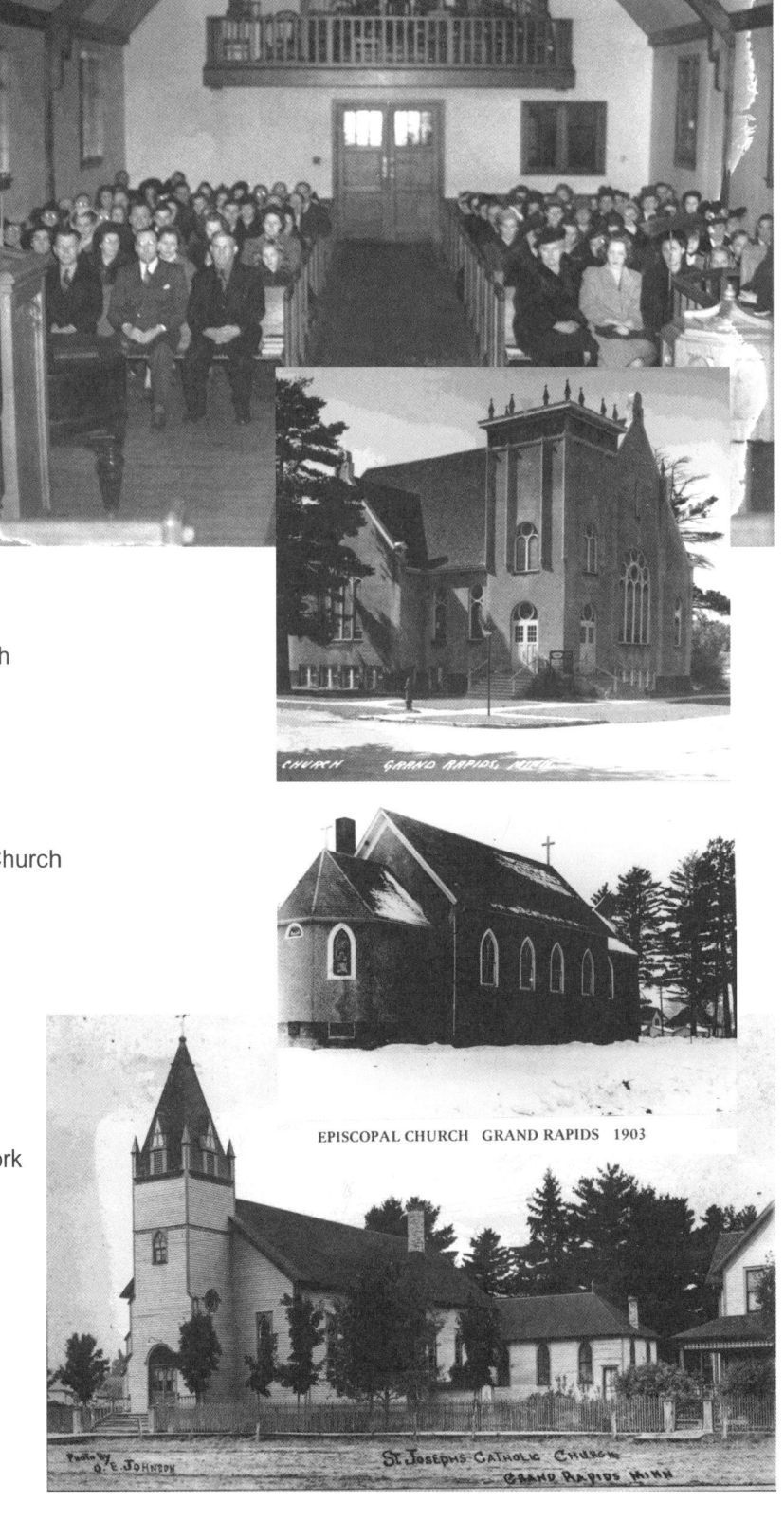

EPISCOPAL CHURCH GRAND RAPIDS 1903

Cohasset
Calvary Pines Baptist Church
Christian Church
Community Bible Chapel
Good News Bible Church
Our Redeemer Lutheran
St. Augustine's Catholic Church
West Cohasset Chapel

Calumet
Calumet Community Presbyterian Church

Coleraine
First United Of Coleraine, Bovey
Mary Immaculate Catholic Church
Methodist Church
Trinity Lutheran

Deer River
Apostolic Faith Ministry
Clara Lutheran
Evangelical Covenant Church
Mission Covenant
Northwoods Chapel
St. Mary's Catholic Church

Effie
Effie Lutheran Church
Presbyterian Effie Church
St. Teresa's Catholic

Marble
Grace English Lutheran
St. Mary's Catholic Church

Marcell
Marcell Community Church

Nashwauk
Nashwauk United Methodist Church

Pengilly
Calvary Baptist Church of Pengilly
Pengilly United Methodist

Warba
Bethel Lutheran
Warba Presbyterian

Country Churches
Alvwood Free Church
Balsam Bible Chapel
Balsam Union Chapel
Centennial Lutheran
Dora Lake Alliance
Goodland Chapel
Grace Lutheran Church
Itasca Bible Church
Jessie Lake Baptist Church
Jessie Lake Lutheran Church
New World Wide Church of God
Northwoods Chapel
Sand Lake Alliance
Scenic Christian Fellowship
Blackberry Seventh Day Adventist Church
Splithand Baptist Church
Suomi Evangelical Lutheran
Trout Lake Apostolic Lutheran

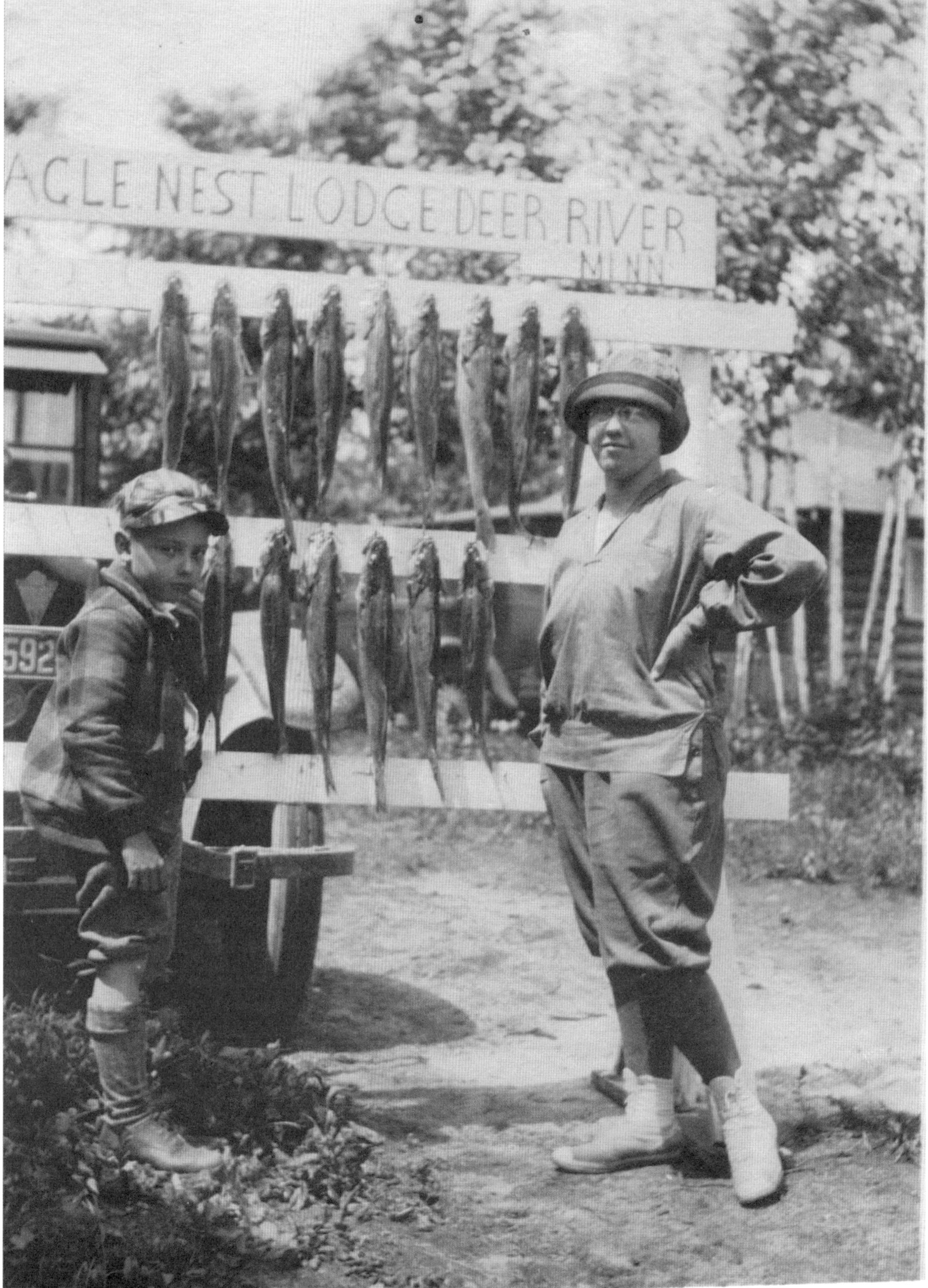
AGLE NEST LODGE DEER RIVER
MINN

ITASCA COUNTY RESORTS

While visiting with Ken Hickman, a writer for the Grand Rapids Herald Review, he presented two leather cases to the Itasca County Historical Society. Each was filled with index cards representing all the Itasca County resorts in the 1940's. This is a list from the collection and includes the camps, some of which eventually became resorts. When Ken toured the resorts he documented the owner's names, some history, how many cabins, and what condition they were in. What he found was that each resort had its own character, their own very faithful customers, and each showcased our natural resources.

RESORTS & CAMPS	LAKE
Allen's	Little Turtle
Allen Camp	Pokegama
Anchor Inn	Little Sand
Arcadia Inn	Turtle
Arrowhead R & G Club	Whitefish
Baker's Place	Bass
Balsam Lodge	Island
Beaver Inn	Rice
Becker's Camp	Turtle
Beth Haven	Pokegama
Big Balsam Camp	Balsam
Big Island Camp	Island
Big Sand	Balsam
Big Too Much Camp	Big Too Much
Big Winnie Camp	Winnibigoshish
Birch Point	Big Ranier
Birchmound	Lawrence
Bittner's	Balsam
Blaha	Busti
Bordash Resort	Balsam
Bowens	Cut Foot Sioux
Bowstring Lodge	Bowstring
Breezy Point	Pokegama
Buck Horn Lodge	Round
Buckhorn	Caribou
Camp Caribou	Caribou
Camp Cregor	Turtle
Camp El Rancho	Shallow
Camp Gould	Gould
Camp Grace	Fox
Camp Idlewild	North Star
Camp Jessie Lake	Jessie
Camp Joyce	Little North Star
Camp Kerr	Bass
Camp Marmac	Johnson
Camp Mayflower	Deer
Camp McGregor	Hatch
Camp Midway	Ball Club

Martin's Resort Trout Lake

Camp Minnesota	Deer
Camp Mishawaka	Pokegama
Camp Pokegama	Pokegama
Camp Vikings	Deer
Camp Warren	Bass
Camp Winakee	Pokegama
Canvas Back Cabins	Round
Cardinal Cottage	Pokegama
Caribou Lake Camp Ground	Caribou
Cedar Point	North Star
Cedar Wild	Moose
Chapel Hills	Sand
Christie's Place	Bowstring
Club House Lake	Club House
Cole's Place	Long
Comfort Cove	Deer
Crystal Springs	Pokegama
Crystal Waters	Johnson
Cut Foot Sioux Inn	Cut Foot Sioux
Cut Foot Sioux Lodge	Cut Foot Sioux
Danola Lodge	Island
Deer Acres	Deer
Dixon Lake	Dixon
Eagle Nest Lodge	Cut Foot Sioux
Edgewater 4 Seasons	Spring
Endahis	Pokegama
Ervin's	Cowhand
Eureka Cabins	Little North Star
Evergreen Lodge	Island
Eze Way Inn	Bowstring
Fairview	Deer
Feltus Place	Prairie
Forest Inn	Round
Ga-Me-Nah-Ego-Co	Dixon
Gill's Landing	Splithand
Government Dam	Winnibigoshish
Graebers Camp	Poverty
Green Rock	Sturgeon
Harrison Resort	Swan
Havenwood	Turtle
Hayslip Corners	Highway 6
Hideaway Inn	Willow
Hoyts	Ann
Huemoellers	Cedar
Indralee	Smith
Ingstad's Resort	Little Turtle
Interlachen Cabins	Deer Lake
Isle View	Pokegama
Itasca Lodge	Rice Lake
Johnson Lake Camp	Johnson
Kananen Brothers	Round
Kents	Balsam Area
Know Us Ark	North Star Lake
Kutina Lodge	Deer

LOBBY AT PINEHURST LODGE, DEER RIVER, MINN.

GALLUP'S RESORT

Lakewood Lodge	Sand
LaPlant's Resort	Pokegama
Little Bass	Little Bass
Little Winnie Lodge	Little Winnie
Lost Lake Camp	Lost
Mackenzie Camp	Turtle
Mallard Point	Prairie
Malvig's Cabin	Busti
Maple Grove	Pokegama
Maple Ridge	Hatch
Marr's Cabins	Pokegama
Martin Place	Spider
McCalls	Balsam
Middle Pidgeon Camp	Middle Pidgeon
Millagan's	Balsam Area
Moody's Bay	Splithand
Moose Lodge	Moose
Murbeck's Cabins	Island
Newstrom's Cabins	Big Ranier
Niska Resort	Round
Nokomis	Little Sand
Northwood Resort	North Star
Oakland Cottages	Big Ole
Otis Lodge	Sugar
Owen Lake Camp	Owen
Patterson	Winnie
Pearson's Lodge	Sand
Penny's Camp	Splithand
Peterson's, C. O.	Moose
Phillips	Little Splithand
Pincherry Grove	Bass
Pine Grove Lodge	Sand
Pinecrest	Third River
Pinecrest	North Star
Pinehurst Lodge	Deer
Prairie Island Camp	Prairie
Red Arrow Lodge	Round
Red Lodge	Round
Resthaven	Round
Resthaven	Gunderson
Rettingers Place	Round
Rudquist Cabins	Dixon
Rush Island Lake	Rush Island
Scenic State Park	Coon
Scenic State Park	Sandwick
Scott's	Sand
Seelye Point Camp	Winnibigoshish
Shady Rest Resort	Little Ball Club
Shallow Lake Resort	Shallow
Six Lake	Fox
Sorgenfrie's	Willow
Steven's	Little Turtle Lake
Sugar Bush Cottages	Bowstring
Summer Haven	Owen Lake

130

The Cedars	Island
Turek's Palce	Horseshoe
Twin Pines	Pokegama
Verndale Cabins	Round
Voight's	Moose
Wa Ga Tha Ka	Wabana
Wabana Lake Lodge	Wabana
Wabigama	Bowstring
Watonga Beach	Smith
Weisert's	Dixon
Wendigo Park	Pokegama
Whispering Pines	Bass
White Birch Inn	Bowstring
Whitten's Camp	Turtle
Wildernessa	Johnson
Wildwood	Pokegama
Wildwood Lodge	Bass
Williams Narrows	Cut Foot Sioux
Willow Lake Hideaway	Willow
Winnie Dam Camp	Winnie Dam
Whispering Pines	Bass
Y-Inn	Highway 46

SUGAR LAKE, GRAND RAPIDS, MINN.—13

131

ITASCA COUNTY SCHOOLS

Again, not all history is whimsical or joyful. But, as a story of all that's remembered, shared, and real, history must tell the tale of what happened.

School shootings in America are not a phenomenon of the 21st century. Nor are they relegated to large cities or well-known locales. The first recorded deliberate school shooting was in 1764. Schoolmaster Enoch Brown and nine children were shot and killed when four Lenape American Indians (aka Delaware Indians) entered the schoolhouse near Greencastle, Pennsylvania brandishing guns.

As would be expected because of the time, with students and teachers carrying firearms for protection during travels to and from remote schools, accidental shootings were bound to occur. But deliberate attempts to harm or kill were a more recent occurrence. This type of tragic crime came to Itasca County in 1916.

Olga Dahl was a single, 23 year old woman raised in Warba who was eager to begin her teaching career at the Round Lake School in Good Hope Township.

In those days, teachers usually roomed with families living near their worksite. Miss Dahl was boarding with the Matt Manula family who lived within walking distance of the Round Lake School. It was there, in the Manula's home, on the morning of September 19th, that an unknown drifter sat at the breakfast table staring at Miss Dahl. Wednesday the 20th would be the third day of classes and the most harrowing day in the life of the young teacher.

Following school that afternoon the new schoolmarm was expected to return to her lodgings at her usual time. When she hadn't arrived by nightfall, nearby residents were contacted but no one had seen her. At daybreak the entire community was alerted via telephone with news of the teacher's disappearance and search parties were organized.

First Central School Building

First Grand Rapids High School

Bearville School

First Forest Lake School

132

First Nashwauk School 1903

Togo School

Island Lake School

Trout Lake Township School

During the extensive search an old woodsman by name of A.A. Clampett noticed evidence of a struggle at the roadside near the school. Investigating the woods a distance from the road, Clampett smelled smoke. Following the scent he came upon a smoldering fire and the body of Miss Dahl. She was tied to a balsam tree and obviously critically injured with gunshot wounds to the head.

She was quickly taken to a nearby house and officials were notified. The doctor who came from Blackduck treated the bullet wound that appeared at the left side of the teacher's face and another that had entered her left temple and penetrated her eye.

But with that, the doctor stopped his ministration. His contention was that the injuries were so extensive that an operation was futile.

Fortunately for Miss Dahl the school had sent for doctors from Grand Rapids and Deer River the following morning. After they completed the necessary surgery, they declared the young teacher's chances for recovery as excellent.

The identity of her assailant would remain unknown for the remainder of 1916 and into the new year even though the perpetrator had apparently left a note at the crime scene:

"This is a pretty friend of hers and she is too pretty for her one [sic] *good so I thing* [sic] *I will fix her so if You Stand happy to find this Boddies* [sic] *I see you later."*

Then in April of 1917 a Round Lake settler made a gruesome discovery along the banks of Dunbar Creek. A revolver lay near the body of a man who had evidently shot a bullet through his own heart. The gun had been discharged three times, accounting for the two wounds suffered by Miss Dahl and the one which took the assailant's life. Numerous people identified the man as the one who had dined at the Manula's table with Miss Dahl the day before he attacked her.

The man was not given the respect of a funeral, but was rather buried where he had fallen on the banks of the creek. Olga eventually recovered, married and with her husband and children returned to Warba. Even with all that transpired, this couldn't be considered a true 'school shooting' since it did not occur on school property although it involved school personnel.

It would be fifty years - almost to the day - before an Itasca County school would know this kind of horror again. However, this time the culmination of events would be more deadly, and with a very different outcome for the perpetrator.

October 5, 1966 broke cold and crisp at Grand Rapids Middle School. Buses had dropped off students who milled around waiting for the bell to announce the start of the school day. Fourteen year old Kevin Roth was one of those students and so was a fifteen year old gunman, David M. Black, Jr.

Black was, by all accounts, an unattractive young man who was very heavy and stood well short of five feet. For these reasons, and probably others, he had been the target of bullies and teasers. To compensate, he would tell outlandish stories about having a moonshine still or a pilot's license, which only fueled the ridicule. Roth revealed in later interviews that he participated in the taunting which may have pushed Black to his extreme actions.

Roth and others stood in front of the school when they saw Black crossing the

Dora Lake School

Cloverdale School

Freestone School

street brandishing a gun. Roth stood motionless as the others scattered. Black suddenly opened fire, hitting Roth in the chest, with the bullet passing through his lungs and other internal organs, lodging in his back.

He stumbled, looking for someone to help. Because he showed no outward signs of bleeding or injury, people ignored or dismissed his pleas, all the while he was bleeding to death internally. He was not the only victim. Immediately after the assault, school administrator, Forrest L. Willey, stepped up. Black then proceeded to shoot Willey in the stomach. It was originally believed that Roth had the most extensive wounds, but it was Willey who died just a week later.

The assault was now categorized as murder and Black's case was moved to adult court with his plea of 'innocent'. Black would change his fate by changing his plea to 'guilty' only days before his jury trial was to commence. That change meant he would be sentenced under Minnesota's Youthful Offender Act. Black was sentenced to 25 years for the killing of Willey. (A 10 year concurrent sentence would also be handed down for the aggravated assault on Roth.)

That, too, would change.

Black served just five years in the state prison at St. Cloud, Minnesota before his

Riverview School

Grand Rapids Middle School 1999

Grand Rapids High School

21st birthday in 1972 when he was paroled.

The Youth Conservation Commission was the paroling authority charged with reviewing juvenile offender cases when the youth reached their 25th birthday. That commission decided to discharge Black's sentence. So, by 1976 Black was free of the corrections system which had charged him with assault and murder.

Roth would recover and return to graduate from Grand Rapids High School. He would go on to complete college and become an educator himself, teaching art and physical education in public schools.

Willey's career and dedication to students and their education was commemorated with a black, granite memorial bench at the Robert J. Elkington Middle School. It was dedicated on October 15, 2013.

Taconite Grade School, 1920s

First Marble School

Deer River High School

SCHOOL   DISTRICT NUMBER

Grand Rapids (GR) Deer River (DR)
Greenway(GW) Nashwauk/Keewatin(NK)

Nashwauk School 1909

School	District
Acropolis	#1 GR
Alder	#6 DR
Alvwood	#1 GR
Anderson	#1 GR
Arbo	#1 GR
Armstrong	#6 DR
Ball Club	#6 DR
Balsam Lake	#1 GR
Balsam "Big" or Smith	#1 GR
Balsam	#1 GR
Bass Lake	#6 DR
Bear River	#1 GR
Bearville	#1 GR
Beighley	#1 GR
Bengal	#1 GR
Bennett	#9 NK
Bergville	#1 GR
Bear	#1 GR
Big Sand	#1 GR
Bigfork	#1 GR
Birchwood	#1 GR
Birdville	#1 GR
Blackberry	#1 GR
Blackberry-Holmberg	#1 GR
Blackie	#1 GR
Bovey	#2 GW
Bowstring	#6 DR
Bridgie	#1 GR
Brock	#1 GR
Buck Lake	#1 GR
Busticogan	#1 GR
Cain	#1 GR
Calumet	#2 GW
Carlson (Pokegama Lake Area)	#1 GR
Carpenter	#1 GR
Central	#1 GR
Clark	#1 GR
Clearwater (Wabana Twp)	#1 GR
Clinite	#1 GR
Cloverdale	#2 GW
Cohasset	#1 GR
Coleraine	#2 GW
Cow	#1 GR
Cowhorn	#1 GR
Cunningham	#1 GR
Daigle	#1 GR
Daybrook	#1 GR
Decker Lake	#1 GR
Deer Lake	#1 GR
Deer River	#6 DR

School	District
Delap-named Spruce Grove	#1 GR
Dell Lake	#1 GR
Demonstration	#1 GR
Dexterville	#1 GR
Diamond Point	#1 GR
Dickens	#1 GR
Dixon Lake Itasca County	#1 GR
Dixon Lake, Rosy, Third River	#1 GR
Donnelly	#6 DR
Dora Lake	#1 GR
Drybridge	#1 GR
Dumas	#6 DR
Dunbar Lake	#1 GR
Dyer	#1 GR
East Ball Club	#6 DR
East Lawrence Lake	#2 GW
East Sand Lake	#6 DR
Edna I. Murphy	#1 GR
Effie	#1 GR
Elmwood	#1 GR
Erven/Erwin Splithand Area	#1 GR
Evergreen	#1 GR
Faulkinghor	#1 GR
Fawn Lake	#6 DR
Feeley	#1 GR
Forest Lake	#1 GR
Forest Lake	#1 GR
Freestone	#1 GR
Garden	#6 DR
Gillon	#6 DR
Goodhope	#1 GR
Goodland	#11 (later #9)
Gran #1	#1 GR
Gran consolidated	#1 GR
Grand Rapids	#1 GR
Grand Rapids High School	#1 GR
Grattan	#1 GR
Grave Lake	#11 & 13
Grave Lake	#6 DR

137

Green Rock	#1 GR		
Greenfield Beach	#6 DR		
Greenway	#2 GW		
Greenwood/Sorenson	#6 DR		
Gustafson	#1 GR		
Hansen Lake	#1 GR		
Hartley	#10		
Harthan	#10		
Harrington	#1 GR		
Harris	#1 GR		
Havens	#1 GR		
Hayden Near Togo	#1 GR		
Hietala/McCloud	#1 GR		
Heywood	#6 DR		
Hill #1	#6 DR		
Hill #2	#6 DR		
Hillcrest	#1 GR		

Trout Lake School circa 1906-1907

Holman	#2 GW	Marcell (open 1919)	#6 DR
Horton	#1 GR	Martin	#1 GR
Houpt	#1 GR	Max	#1 GR
Hulbert	#6 DR	McCloud	#1 GR
Inger	#6 DR	McCormick	#1 GR
Island Lake- mail Calumet	#1 GR	McDonald	#6 DR
Island Lake	#1 GR	McIntire/McGuire	#1 GR
Island Lake	#1 GR	McKinley (became Liebrick 1916)	#1 GR
Jackson	#6 DR	McLeod	#1 GR
Jaynes	#6 DR	McMahon	#1 GR
Jessie Lake #1	#6 DR	Moose Creek	#1 GR
Jessie Lake #2	#6 DR	Moose Lodge	#6 DR
Kananen NW Itasca Co	#1 GR	Moose Park	#1 GR
Keewatin	#9 NK	Nashwauk	#9 NK
Keewatin High	#9 NK	Nashwauk High	#9 NK
Keewatin-Nashwauk Jr. High	#9 NK	Nashwauk-Keewatin High	#9 NK
Kennedy	#6 DR	Nass	#1 GR
Kinghurst	#1 GR	Nelson near Alvwood	#1 GR
Knaeble	#1 GR	Noble NW Itasca Co	#1 GR
LaPrairie	#2 GW	North/Island	#5 DR
Larson	#1 GR	North Jessie	#6 DR
Leighton Brook	#10	North School consolidated	#6 DR
Leipold	#1 GR	Northland	#1 GR
Lepisto	#1 GR	Northwest	#1 GR
Liberty/Wirt	#1 GR	Olcott-Marble	#2 GW
Liebrick near Wendigo	#1 GR	O'Leary near Nashwauk	#1 GR
Link Lake (burned down)	#1 GR	Orchid	#1 GR
Link Lake	#1 GR	Orsenfeld	#1 GR
Little Sand Lake	#6 DR	Orth	#1 GR
Little Turtle Lake	#6 DR	Ottum Bigfork Valley area	#1 GR
Lower Balsam	#1 GR	Paratala	#1 GR
Maher/Wabasse	#5 DR	Pengilly	#2 GW
Mahoner	#1 GR	Phillip Murray Bovey	#2 GW
Maki	#1 GR	Pine Grove	#1 GR
Maple Grove NW Itasca Co.	#1 GR	Pinecrest	#12
Marble/Olcott	#2 GW	Pinecrest	#1 GR
Marble Elementary	#2 GW	Pinetop	#1 GR
Marcell (open 1906)	#6 DR	Plum Creek	#1 GR

138

Pogue	#1 GR		
Pokegama (open 1901)	#1 GR		
Pokegama	#1 GR		
Pomroy	#1 GR		
Poplar Grove/Franklin	#6 DR		
Popple	#1 GR		
Popple River	#1 GR		
Rahier	#1 GR		
Range Line	#1 GR		
Reed Lake	#1 GR		
Reed/Rose	#6 DR		
Rice Lake	#1 GR		
Rice Rapids	#10		
Riverview	#1 GR		
Robertson NW Itasca Co	#1 GR		
Robinson	#1 GR		
Rock Creek	#1 GR	Swanson School	#1 GR
Rosy/Decker	#1 GR	Taconite	#2 GW
Round Lake	#1 GR	Teesaker NW Itasca Co	#1 GR
Russell	#6 DR	Third River NW Itasca Co	#1 GR
St. Paul School	#9 NK	Third River NW Itasca Co	#12
Sand Lake	#6 DR	Thorofare	#1 GR
Sand Lake/Pogue Feeley twp	#1 GR	Thydean	#6 DR
Scenic Park	#1 GR	Tichenor (open 1905)	#1 GR
Schumacher	#1 GR	Tichenor	#1 GR
Shafer	#1 GR	Tick	#1 GR
Shallow Pond	#1 GR	Togo	#1 GR
Shoal Lake	#1 GR	Trout Lake (open 1895)	#1 GR
Saizer/Sizer	#1 GR	Trout Lake (open 1916)	#1 GR
Smith	#1 GR	Trout Lake	#2 GW
Sombs	#6 DR	Tydean	#6 DR
South	#5 (later #1)	Vance	#1 GR
South Bigfork	#6 DR	Verna	#1 GR
South Bowstring	#6 DR	Warba (4 schools)	#1 GR
Southwest	#1 GR	Wabana	#1 GR
Spang	#1 GR	Wautona	#1 GR
Splithand old log school	#1 GR	Wawina 4 diff. schools	#1 GR
Splithand	#1 GR	Welch Lake #1	#1 GR
Spring Lake	#6 DR	Welch Lake #2	#1 GR
Spruce Grove	#1 GR	Welte	#1 GR
Spruce Park	#1 GR	Wendigo	#1 GR
Squaw Lake consolidated	#1 GR	West Bigfork	#6 DR
Squaw Lake	#1 GR	West Lawrence Lake	#2 GW
Stingy Lake	#1 GR	West Moose Park	#1 GR
Stonefield	#1 GR	West Oteneagen	#6 DR
Sturgeon Lake	#1 GR	Westfork	#1 GR
Sugar Lake	#1 GR	White Oak	#10
Sundloff/Turtle	#6 DR	Whitefish Lake	#6 DR
Sunrise Balsam Area	#1 GR	Wirt	#6 DR
Suomi	#6 DR	Wolfe NW Itasca Co	#1 GR
Suomi	#5	Woodview	#1 GR
Suomi	#13	Vandyke Coleraine	#2 GW
Suomi Gram Lake	#1 GR	Zaiser	#1 GR
Swan River	#1 GR	Zemple	#6 DR
Swanson School	#6 DR		

McMahon School

SHERIFFS

Few county positions contain more intriguing stories than that of sheriff.

An act of the legislature detached Itasca County from Aitkin County and organized it as a separate county and provided for election of officers. In 1891, Governor William Merriman appointed a county board. This board was given authority to appoint county officials to serve until the next election. There was one exception. The sheriff of Aitkin County, Joseph M. Markham, was to serve as Itasca County sheriff until the next election. He served until Mike Toole was officially elected in November of 1892.

Fifty years after a war of words leading to the cowardly murder of an unarmed man in La Prairie, the entire world was at war. There was now a page in the history of Itasca County for Deputy Sheriff, Otto Litchke. His name would be written in connection with two Nazi prisoners of war. And their story would happen in the heart of Itasca County.

In 1944 a former Civilian Conservation Corps Camp near Bena housed a number of Nazi prisoners. It was one of the World War II prisoner of war camps in Northern Minnesota, along with Cut Foot Sioux, Day Lake and Remer.

On October 29, 1944 Nazi Corporal Heinz Schymalla and Walter Mai, captured in 1943 in Tunisia, escaped their camp.

Having supplied a small boat they called 'Lili Marlene No. 10', after a German folk ballad, they used a small map showing the connection of Lake Winnibigoshish to the Mississippi River (and on to New Orleans) to set a course. Unfortunately for them, they missed the Mississippi River turn off, having taken a wrong turn into Jay Gould Lake. J.G. Shoup, a resort owner, came upon them having lunch on the shoreline. That's when Itasca County Deputy Sheriff, Otto Litchke, was notified. After a slow search of the area, the two escapees surrendered and were sentenced to thirty days confinement. Litchke had just apprehended two of the thirteen German prisoners who escaped from prisoner of war camps in Minnesota during World War II.

"Prisoners of War in lunchroom, prisoners of war camp near Deer River"
From Minneapolis Tribune, March 4, 1945. Photo Roy Swan.
Print copied from collections of the Minnesota Historical Society.

This all happened long after County Sheriff, William Hoolihan, had retired. During his service from 1902 to 1908 he was summoned to Nashwauk where miners were striking. Hoolihan brought along a sufficient number of deputies and that show of force was enough to maintain order.

Before he was elected as Sheriff, Hoolihan had been a lumberjack of note. He had been a foreman of large camps for Itasca Lumber Company. Throughout his three terms he was known as the "lumberjack Sheriff".

The Aitkin County Sheriff, Joseph M. Markham, was appointed Itasca County Sheriff in March 1891, until an official election was held in November 1892. Michael L. Toole was elected. The term for sheriff was for two years and candidates filed for the office with a party designation.

Michael L. Toole
January 1893 to
December 1898
Served 6 years

William Tyndall
January 1899 to
December 1902
Served 4 years

William M. Hoolihan
January 1903 to
December 1908
Served 6 years

Thomas T. Riley
January 1909 to
December 1914
Served 6 years

In November 1912 election, the term for sheriff and other county officials was changed to 4 years and candidates filed for office without any party affiliation.

Charles Gunderson
January 1915 to
December 1918
Served 4 years

Edward J. Carson
January 1919 to
December 1922
Served 4 years

George O'Brien
January 1923 to
December 1926
Served 4 years

Howard A. Harmond
January 1927 to
December 1930
Served 4 years

Elmer Madson
January 1931 to
December 1938
Served 8 years

William Crisp
January 1939 to
December 1946
Served 8 years

Marvin W. Mitchell
January 1947 to
December 1962
Served 16 years

John P. Muhar
January 1963 to
December 1974
Served 12 years

Russell Johannsen
January 1975 to
December 1990
Served 16 years

Robert Serich
January 1991 to
December 1994
Served 4 years

Pat Medure
January 1995 to
December 2010
Served 16 years

Victor Williams
January 2011 to ...

Potatoe Festival featuring the "Spud Dog"

Publications In Research Center at Itasca County Historical Society

History of Arbo Township by Esther Hietala.
Bear River Heritage Book by Frances K. Scofield & Judith Blyckert; Copyrighted 1986 by Judith A. Blyckert; published August 1986
Looking Back – A History of Finns in Balsam by Alvar E. Hupila
Balsam Township by Alvar E. Hupila; Copyrighted in 2006
Minn Farm Homesteads of Bass Lake,. Vol 1, by Donald J. Rydrych; Copyright in June 1998; Printed by Inland Printing Co., Walla Walla, Washington
The Log White House by Mabel White; First Printing
Our Story-History of People of Bass Brook Township by Patricia Grimsbo, Compiler; First Printing—March 1984
Trails Through the Northwoods by Patricia Navratil; Copyrighted in 1976 by Northwoods Press, Inc.; Printed by Northwoods Press, Bigfork MN
Bigfork Valley Memories Volume I by David Patrow; Copyrighted in 1989 by David Patrow
Bigfork Valley Memories Volume II by David Patrow; Published November 1992; Copyrighted in 1992 by David M. Patrow
On the Banks of the Bigfork by Dorothy Manske; Copyrighted in 1976 by Northwoods Press; Printed by Northwoods Press Inc., Bigfork , MN
Bigfork High by Bigfork High School
Prosper, Can You Tell Me More? by Leo Trunt; Copyright in 1993 by Leo Trunt; Published by Gateway Press, Inc.,1001 N Calvert Street, Baltimore, MD 21202
Beyond the Circle by Leo Trunt; Copyrighted in 1998 by Leo Trunt and Printed by Gateway Press, Inc., 1001 N Calvert Street, Baltimore, MD 21202
Bigfork Minnesota Centennial by Centennial Book Committee
Bovey: A Century of Change by Donald L. Boese and Patricia J. Walls; Published by the City of Bovey, MN in 2004 and Printed and designed by Rapids Printing, Grand Rapids MN
Bovey: A Century of Change II by Donald L. Boese and Patricia J. Walls; Printed by Rapids Printing, Grand Rapids, MN in 2011
100 Years Bovey Farmers Day by Donald L. Boese and Patricia J. Walls; Printed by Rapids Printing, Grand Rapids, MN in 2011
Itasca Centennial by Bovey Press; Published by Bovey Press in Bovey MN
Back to Buck Lake by S. Lowell Roberts; Copyright in 1993 by Edgar J. Brooks and Allie Brooks; Published by Eastern Itascan Company, 310 Central Avenue, Nashwauk, MN 55769
Calumet Golden Jubilee by Golden Jubilee Committee; Published by the Calumet MN Golden Jubilee Committee
Calumet Diamond Jubilee by Diamond Jubilee Committee;
Restoration Plan - Old Calumet, Minnesota
Going Back Down Memory Lane by Helen Steinberg Adamson
Carnegie Public Library (Coleraine)
Coleraine Jubilee by Coleraine Diamond Jubilee
The DeCoster Place on Deer Lake by Cyrus DeCoster
The Lake of Changing Colors by Cyrus DeCoster; Copyrighted in 2000 by Barbara DeCoster and Printed by Adams Press, 500 North Michigan Avenue, Suite 1920, Chicago, Illinois, 60611
Cyrus King – The Sage of Deer River by Brian Vroman;
Deer River Yesterday and Today by Deer River Federated Woman's Club; Compiled by Deer River Federated Woman's Club as late as August, 1973; Printed by Craft Printing by Darrell R. Emerson, 312 4th Street SE Deer River, MN 56636
Deer River Area Centennial History by Deer River Area Centennial Committee; Copyright in March 1998 by Deer River Centennial Committee; Printed by Deer River Publishing, Deer River MN in March 1998
Deer River Centennial – 100 Years in 1998
A Distant Record (Northome) by Carol Ann Lundberg; Copyrighted in 2010 and Published by One Loon Press, 65629 County Road 174, Northhome, MN 56661
Pengilly History and Memories by Barb Shipka; Printed by Express Print One, Ltd. Hibbing, MN
Rest of the Story (Pengilly) by Barb Shipka
Voices of Pokegama by Ann K. Ryan; Copyrighted in 2005 by the Greater Pokegama Lake Association—First Edition; Published by Greater Pokegama Lake Association
A History of Oklahoma Hill, Deer Lake, Minnesota by Dorothy Miller
Yesterday by Eleanor Otis; Copyrighted in 1985 by Eleanor Otis
Memories of Spring Lake, Minnesota by Eugene Heide
Stingy Lake Country by Mary Spotts; Copyrighted in 1988 by Mary Emma Spotts; Printed by The Eastern Itascan Printing and Publishing Co., Nashwauk MN 55769
Remembering Rosy by Esther (Johnson) Connell; Copyrighted in 2001 by Esther (Johnson) Connell and Published by Hill Top Publishing, 6913 Gleason Circle, Edina, MN 55439-1600
The Challenge of Sissebakwet by Arthur R. Otis; Copyrighted in 1976 by Arthur R. Otis
50 Years and more of Suomi by Historical Committee of Suomi; Compiled in 1967 for the 50th anniversary celebration
Taconite Diamond Jubilee by Diamond Jubilee Planning Committee
The Third River Story – A Nice Place in the Woods by Third River Historical Group; Produced by The Third River Historical Group; Printed by Presto Print, Grand Rapids, MN in 2002

Oh Wawina – A Decade Gone By 1999-2000 by Wawina Community Activities Club; Planned and produced by the 1999-2000 Wawina Community Acivities Historical Booklet Committee; Copyrighted in 2000
Wawina Centennial History Book 2000-2010 by Wawina Community Activities Club
Oh Wawina From Then Til Now by Wawina Community Activities Club (1990); Copyrighted in 1990
60 Years of Progress – The Itasca Campus by Barbara Sanderson
Odds and Ends – Itasca County History by Brian Vroman
Taconite Centennial Celebration 1907-2007 by Taconite Centennial Committee;
Sago Saga by Gert Montague; Copyrighted in 1989 by Gert Montague; Printed in USA
Precious Memories - The History of Spang Community by Stan Watson
Along Memory Trails (Deer River) by Gladys Erola; Published by The Western Itasca Review in Deer River, MN
Homestead Days by Effie Bicentennial Committee
One Mans Journey Through the Swamps of Good Hope by Emil Johnson; The Copyrights are reserved by children of Emil Johnson and future gernerations
Celebrating a Century of Good Hope by Emil and Irene Maki Johnson; Printed by Minuteman Press, Grand Rapids, MN
Logging Town by WPA Writers Program; Copyrighted in 1941 by Village of Grand Rapids, MN; Printed Second Printing in 1978 by the Itasca County Historical Society
Last of the Giants by Harry Rimmer; Copyright 1948 by Research Science Bureau, Inc.;
Grand Rapids and Itasca – Looking Back the Early Years by Herald Review and ICHS; Copyright 2004; Published by Pediment Publishing
Grand Rapids Companion 1891-1991   by Centennial Committee
Harris Township Centennial by Peggy Bishop
Itasca County People Study Their Land by Itasca County; Report made in June 1942
Itasca County - the Coming Country by Itasca County
Jessie Lake the First Fifty Years by Olga Lindgren Wise; First Printing: November 2001; Second Printing: January 2002
Grand Rapids Bicentennial Showcase 1776-1976
Keewatin Centennial 2006 by Ann Michelich and Dr. Dan P. Kelley
Early Settlers at Island Lake by Leila S. Atwood; Compiled by Leila S. Atwood
Itasca County - It's Fair, Agricultural Association and Agriculture by Brian M. Carlson; Copyright in 1993 by Itasca County Historical Society; Printed by NorthPrint International, Grand Rapids, MN
Itasca Nursing Home – 100 Years of Service by Donna Kersting & Brian M. Carlson; Published by Scenic Range News, Bovey, MN
LaPrairie - the Road Back by Dick Cain; Copyright in 1990 by the City of LaPrairie, LaPrairie, MN
Golden Jubilee Marble by Souvenir Booklet Committee; Printed by the Eastern Itascan, Nashwauk, MN and Published in 1958
Northwoods Pioneers by WPA Project
Incomplete History of the Area South of Marble by Verna (Poppe) Bossen
Marble Centennial Celebration by Centennial Committee;
Marble Diamond Jubilee by Diamond Jubilee Committee
History of Marcell Community Church by Curtis L Newstrom
Memories of a Small Town – Marcell by Curtis L. Newstrom; Published by Curtis L. Newstrom in 1995 and Printed by The Printery, Clay Center, Kansas
No Place Like Max by Bernard Anderson and Tom Boeder
Nashwauk – 50th Anniversary by 50th Anniversary Book Committee; Published in 1953 by The Eastern Itascan, Nashwauk, MN; Compiled by the Fiftieth Anniversary Book Committee
Nashwauk – From Timber to Taconite by 75th Anniversary Book Committee; Published in 1978 by The Eastern Itascan, Nashwauk, MN
My Old Hometown (Nashwauk) by Centennial Book Committee
Memories of Nashwauk - My Old Hometown by Centennial Book Committee; Compiled in Spring of 2005
Northome Community Centennial History by Faye M. Estabrooks; Copyrighted in 2003 and Printed by The Northhome Record and Published by Northwoods Craft, Inc.
Papermakers by Don Boese; Copyright in 1984 by the Charles K. Blandin Foundation, Grand Rapids, MN; Manufactured in USA
Timber Connections by Susan Hawkinson & Warren Jewett; Copyright 2013 by Susan Hawkinson and Warren Jewett; Bluewaters Press, Box 246, Grand Rapids, MN 55744
Tim-BERRR! Pine Logging in the Bigfork River Country, Vols 1 & 2 by Benhart Rajala; Vol 1: Copyright 1991; Vol 2:1992; North Star Press of St. Cloud, MN

We also have books covering the following subjects: Native Americans, logging and paper, mining, transportation, rivers and lakes, military, plat books, family histories and fiction and non-fiction by local authors.

Other resources include manuscript files, county newspapers and census records on microfilm, yearbooks, obituary records, phone books, cemetery records and thousands of photos. We also have access to *Ancestry.com* for the public to use.

GLOSSARY

Band – division following the same sign; a group of people joined together for a common purpose

Charter School – a school that receives public funding but operates independently of the public school system in which it is located

City – center of population larger than town or village

Community – group of people living together

Contract post office – an "approved postal provider" that's operated by a private business or community and not staffed by United States Postal Service (USPS) workers and doesn't offer the full range of services and products

Dough Boy – a United States infantryman

Ethnonym – names applied to a given ethnic group that can be used interchangeably

Etymologist – an expert on the branch of linguistics that deals with the origin and development of words

Grippe – earlier term for influenza (flu)

Indian – any of the aboriginal peoples (American Indian) of North or South America, or the West Indies, or of the culture

Ku Klux Klan – secret society organized in Atlanta Georgia in 1915 to reestablish and maintain white supremacy: it is anti-Negro, anti-Semitic, anti-Catholic etc.

Log boom – an area in which logs are confined

Mennonite – member of an evangelical Protestant Christian sect who favor plain living and oppose the taking of oaths, infant baptism, military service and accepting public office

Millinery – a place where they design, make, trim, or sell women's hats

Ojibwe – also spelled Ojibwa or Ojibway is an ethnonym for Chippewa and Anishinabe

Plat – a map of a piece of land divided into building lots

Polio – an acute infectious disease caused by virus inflammation of gray matter of the spinal cord

Quasquicentenial – marking 125 years

Reservation – public land set aside for some special use

Rough Riders – a volunteer cavalry regiment organized by Theodore Roosevelt for service in the Spanish-American War

Sioux – same as Dakota Indians

Sluice – artificial passage for water with a gate or valve to regulate flow

Small Pox – an acute, highly contagious virus disease

Spur – a short side track connected with the main track of a railroad

Suspension bridge – bridge suspended from chains or cables anchored at either end and supported by towers at regular intervals

Taconite – low-grade iron ore pelletized for blast-furnace reduction

Town – group of houses larger than village

Township – division of a county constituting a unit of local government with administrative control over schools, roads etc

Treaty – a legally binding agreement between two separate sovereign nations

Tribe – group of persons, families, or clans forming a close community under a leader or chief

Village – incorporated community smaller than city or town

Women's suffrage – political movement that advocated the right of women to vote

Dam Break 1949 at Blandin Paper Company

Karjala History Research Center

What will you leave behind for future generations? What will be your legacy?

Waino and Marie Karjala answered those questions by endowing every citizen in Itasca County with a Historical Research Center.

Waino and Marie were brother and sister dairy farmers in Trout Lake Township. Their father had come to America in 1905 from the Kajaani region in Finland and their mother, whose maiden name was Pyykkonen, in 1907 from the same area. Hard working immigrants, the couple bought fifty-eight acres in Trout Lake which son, Waino, grew to 160 acres.

It was Waino and his sister Marie who developed the dairy herd.

Teddy Roosevelt was U.S. President when Waino was born in 1908. By 1910 when Marie was born, the president was William Howard Taft.

Neither Waino nor Marie ever married or had children.

The pair took part in Itasca County Historical Society history tour of Bovey and Coleraine which was hosted by Itasca Community College historian, Don Boese. That sparked their interest in expanding the availability of historical information and research to everyone.

In 1995, the Karjalas established an endowment for that purpose.

Located within the Itasca County Historical Society in Grand Rapids, the Karjala History Research Center is a vast collection of information and histories related to Itasca County. Anyone can access the maps and atlases; high school yearbooks; photographic records; newspapers on microfilm; United States and foreign research books; cemetery records and obituaries; and family and oral histories. It also offers computer access to *Ancestry.com* and is staffed by knowledgeable volunteers and staff who offer research assistance.

Consider leaving a portion of your estate to Itasca County Historical Society or establish a "fund" through the Grand Rapids Area Community Foundation.

If you aren't able to leave an endowment, at least leave your history. Someone you will never know will thank you in the future.

Marie Karjala
1910-2002

Waino Karjala
1908-1998

Contact ICHS by phone: 218-326-6431 or email: ichs@paulbunyan.net for further Information on leaving your legacy.